"As a long-time lover of C. S. Lewis and the world of Narnia, I have read countless books about both. Joe Rigney's *Live Like a Narnian* is one of the best. It overflows with an authentic sense of Narnian brightness, wisdom, and wonder. Rigney seems equally at home with Lewis's fiction and nonfiction. He draws them together beautifully, with truth and imagination. I highly recommend this delightful book!"

   RANDY ALCORN, author of *Heaven* and *If God Is Good*; Director of Eternal Perspectives Ministries

"Joe Rigney is a writer who really knows how to love something. I am glad that he loves Narnia."

   DOUGLAS WILSON, author of *What I Learned in Narnia* and *Father Hunger*; Pastor, Christ Church, Moscow, ID

"In our journey to Aslan's Country, we tend to look to the right and to the left to see who's coming with us. There is much to share, and in the sharing, we feel the fullness of resolution and the resolution of fullness. This book is stuffed full of the must-share Narnian "Aha!" moments that keep you turning just one more page. Even the moments you've only whispered to yourself about. I'm betting that *Live Like a Narnian* will prove to be a trusted companion to future Narnians who will read and re-read the Chronicles for generations."

   GLORIA FURMAN, author of *Glimpses of Grace*, daughter of Eve, and a queen of Narnia

"*Live Like a Narnian* has the quality that all good writing strives for: it is both insightful and delightful. Joe Rigney captures not only the power and poignancy of C. S. Lewis's beloved Narnia series, but also its fun and merriment."

   DEVIN BROWN, author of *A Life Observed: A Spiritual Biography of C. S. Lewis*; Professor of English, Asbury University

"It has been said that what C. S. Lewis thought about everything was secretly present in what he wrote about anything, and so it's no surprise to discover in his Narnia the sweeping worldview he detailed in his non-fiction prose. This world Lewis created is shot through with theological riches, put there like veins of gold running through a Colorado Mountain. I have long awaited a brief book that labors to excavate the major theological themes in Narnia in a simple and clear format, a book that calls on Lewis's nonfiction writings as a commentary to illuminate his Narnian stories, and most of all, a book about that bright gold creature more terrible and more beautiful than anything in all of Narnia and this world combined. The wait is over. *Live Like a Narnian* by Joe Rigney is a masterful achievement."

TONY REINKE, author of *Lit! A Christian Guide to Reading Books*; Content Strategist at desiringGod.org

"It's evident that Joe Rigney has deeply breathed the air of Narnia for a long time, and he creatively applies Lewis's masterpiece to Christian living with wit and wisdom."

ANDY NASELLI, editor of *Themelios* Journal; Assistant Professor of New Testament, Biblical Theology, Bethlehem College and Seminary

"Halfway through reading *Live Like a Narnian*, the chapters had already had their intended effect and deepened my appreciation and understanding of Narnia. They made me want to slow down, savor them, and keep learning from them while breathing anew the Narnian air one more time. I heartily commend this book to you."

MATTHEW LEE ANDERSON, author of *The End of Our Exploring: A Book About Questioning and the Confidence of Faith*; Lead Writer at MereOrthodoxy.com

"The immediate effect of *Live Like a Narnian*: I want to. Written with a fun, lively, muscular style, it succeeds both as a work of popular literary criticism and as a readable call to follow Aslan all the way to the end. If you want to recover the wisdom and beauty of the original Narnia, that vision that captivated so many of us in our youth and that continues to work its edifying magic, dive into Joe Rigney's stirring introduction."

OWEN STRACHAN, Assistant Professor of Christian Theology and Church History, Boyce College; author, *Risky Gospel: Abandon Fear and Build Something Awesome*

Live Like a Narnian

Christian Discipleship in Lewis's Chronicles

Joe Rigney

ISBN: 0615872042
ISBN-13: 978-0615872049

Eyes & Pen Press
Minneapolis, Minnesota

Designed and typeset by Matt Crutchmer.
Printed by CreateSpace.

To Sam and Peter
May You Always Be True Sons of Archenland:
First In, Last Out, and Laughing Loudest

CONTENTS

Acknowledgments

This book was produced in an unusually short amount of time (six months from start to finish), though it had been banging around in my head for a few years. The quick turnaround from conception to completion means that many thanks are due to many people. For starters, I'd like to thank C. S. Lewis for writing the books, and my parents for introducing them to me when I was a kid. I don't recall my first reading of the book, but I did find my childhood copies. The pages are as well-worn as one would expect.

No one was more instrumental in moving this book from idea to print than my friend David Mathis. He encouraged me to take the risk and then worked alongside me: editing, encouraging, strategizing, and promoting the book in countless ways. I'm grateful to God for David's friendship (and to his wife Meg for allowing him to spend a few late nights reading the manuscript). Matt Crutchmer is responsible for the entirety of the design of the book, from the cover to the page layout to the typeface selection, and I couldn't be more pleased with his work. Matt is a tremendous graphic designer, a thoughtful theologian, and a true friend of Narnia (though he is a die-hard fan of soccer, which, as everyone knows, is the national sport of Calormen).

Bryan DeWire offered his capable eye to proofreading, formatting, and looking up citations. His enthusiasm for the project only served to increase my own, and I'm grateful he was willing to lend a hand. Tony Reinke and Dave Clifford at Desiring God were early and persistent encouragers of this project. Tony reads and reviews a lot of books, and his enthusiastic endorsement was a gift from God at the right time. Dave was crucial in thinking strategically about the book, and he graciously allowed me to promote the book at the Desiring God National Conference. In that vein, I'm grateful to John Piper and Scott Anderson for inviting me to speak on Narnia at the conference on Lewis. Without that invitation, I wouldn't have spent all of those late nights and early mornings writing and re-writing this book.

I'm grateful to God for my colleagues at Bethlehem College and Seminary—Ryan Griffith, Johnathon Bowers, and Josh Maloney—who encouraged me to pursue the project, despite our busy academic schedule. Our faculty team is a reminder that, *contra* Miraz, it is possible to have more than one king at a time. Additionally, I'm profoundly grateful to the BCS students who came to my house each week in April and May 2013 for "Pizza in Narnia." During those evenings, we'd eat Little Caesar's, I'd read the latest drafts of the chapters, and the students would ask questions and give valuable feedback. Without those weekly "deadlines," this book would not have been written (I knew that if I didn't write something, we'd have to sit around and stare at each other over $5 pizza). So to Nick Aufenkamp, Eric Satterfield, Amber Doran, Alen Anthrayose, Wil Anderson, Keith Kresge, Courtney Young, Clayton Hutchins, Ivy White, Andrew Kasahara, Ren Carolino, James and Lexi Nelson, Tyler Pierson, James Carr, Juan Abreu, Nick Sevier, Melissa O'Neill, Andrew Horning, Zack Melvin, Ryan McLaughlin, Amanda Sutton, Mark O'Neill, the Green family, Christina Hall, Cody and Whitney Sandidge (I think that's everyone): Thank you.

I'm grateful to others who read various iterations of this book and encouraged it along the way: Zach and Betsy Howard, Jason

Abell, Andy Naselli, Doug Wilson, Matthew Lee Anderson, Owen Strachan, Devin Brown, Gloria Furman, Randy Alcorn, and Nick Laparra.

My wife Jenny enthusiastically supported this project, despite the fact that she would "lose" me many evenings so that I could write, re-write, edit, and perform a thousand other book-related activities. She's also the inspiration for the final chapter on the Glory of a Narnian Queen, and those who read that chapter and know her will no doubt detect the resemblance.

Finally, I'm grateful to God for my two boys, Sam and Peter, knights-in-training (or as we like to say around our house, "the Protectors"). It was a great joy for me to read *The Lion, the Witch, and the Wardrobe* to Sam for the first time while this book was being written. His nightly recaps of the story to my wife were priceless. Reading Narnia and writing this book have only stoked my desire to raise both of my sons to be the kind of men who cheerfully embrace whatever adventures Aslan sends them. It's to them that I dedicate this book.

A Word to the Reader

This book was written for friends of narnia. In the author's judgment, its usefulness is in direct proportion to one's familiarity with the Chronicles. All of the chapters assume that the reader knows the characters in the books, the basic plot of each story, and key scenes and quotations, among other things. While no doubt some may be able to derive benefit from it without prior knowledge of Narnia, I'd recommend against it, both because without such knowledge the reader will be confused, and because I do not wish to prejudice readers should they finally enter the wardrobe themselves. I believe that what I've written here is true, and faithful to Lewis's intentions. However, I much prefer people to read these chapters and say, "Ah, yes. That's exactly what I've always thought about that scene, or that character, or that theme," than to take what I've written and go on a hunt for it somewhere in the Western Wild.

To those who consider themselves free Narnians and sons of Archenland, in the name of the Lion, welcome. In no way is this book intended to be a substitute for reading the actual books for the seventeenth time (though I do hope they enrich the seventeenth reading). Stories are irreducibly stories; you cannot boil them down into essays, no matter how true or accurate the essays (and I do hope these essays exceed those that Lewis disparages in *The Horse and His Boy*). Flannery O'Connor said somewhere that a story is a way to say something that can't be said any other way, and it takes every word in the story to say what the meaning is. Lewis is a master of such narratival, tacit, and implicit communication. His way of "describing-around" something leaves a deeper imprint than any essay can hope to.

At the same time, I hope that these chapters will cause some lights to go on in your soul (and maybe even a rocket to go up inside your head). And while I'm thinking about it, some readers may find the Introduction overly technical and complicated. If that's you, I give my glad permission to skip ahead and get right into the chapters; they're more fun anyway. Also, it's worth noting that, in order to accommodate the various editions of the Chronicles, I've chosen to cite book and chapter number rather than page number. Since most of my chapters are focused on only one Chronicle, you'll often only find a chapter number in parentheses. Hopefully it won't be too confusing.

Finally, while I would discourage giving this book to children *directly* (just give them Narnia; when they're older they can read these chapters to learn some of what Narnia has been doing to them), I do hope that my modest efforts will benefit them in a roundabout way. In particular, I'd like Christian parents to come away eager to intentionally read the stories to their children, in hope that another generation will be shaped, molded, and matured into men and women of God, the kind that resemble the Lion of Narnia, and therefore, bear the image of the true king, Jesus Christ.

Introduction

Learning to Breathe Narnian Air

Discipleship and the Shaping Power of Stories

In 1956, after completing the last book in the Chronicles of Narnia, C. S. Lewis wrote a short article in the *New York Times Book Review* explaining how a childless Professor of Medieval and Renaissance Literature came to write fairy tales.

Dismissing the idea that he had some master plan to "say something about Christianity to children" which led him to choose the fairy tale genre, research the reading habits of children, select some Christian doctrines, and then write allegories, Lewis writes,

> Everything began with images; a faun carrying an umbrella, a queen on a sledge, a magnificent lion. At first there wasn't anything Christian about them; that element pushed itself in of its own accord. It was part of the bubbling.[1]

This "bubbling" produced some of the most beloved children's tales in all of literature. Thousands of young children have lain in their beds and begged their parents for "just one more chapter." Older children have devoured entire books (sometimes two or three at a time) over a long, lazy Saturday. College students have successfully avoided studying for that big exam simply by noticing the books on a shelf and setting off to find that one line about "not being a tame lion." Even some middle-aged adults have been known to disappear for entire afternoons only to emerge with a wistful sigh from who-knows-where murmuring something about "Beaversdam, fried trout, and sticky marmalade rolls."

I confess to being all of these people (though I'm not quite middle-aged yet), and I think my time spent reading, dreaming, thinking, and talking about hospitable fauns, singing stars, evil witches, and a certain Lion has not been in the least wasted. And not merely because reading fictional stories is a healthy part of recreation and refreshment (which it certainly is). Had Lewis written his stories in Moses's day, I have no doubt that Narnia would have been recommended reading on the Sabbath.

Meeting God in Narnia

My reason for viewing my hours (and days and years) in Narnia as time well spent is that I firmly believe that I am a better husband, better father, better friend, better teacher, better son and brother—in sum, a better man and Christian—because of it. Living in Narnia has profoundly shaped my view of society, culture, marriage, parenting, education, and theology. (And when I say Narnia has shaped me, I am implicitly including Lewis's other writings as well, for as his friend Owen Barfield once said—and I hope to demonstrate in this book—"what Lewis thought about everything was secretly present in what he said about anything."[2])

I have met God—the true God, the living God, the Father of Jesus Christ—in and through the bubbling that Lewis called Narnia, and I have grown in my love and affection for Jesus through breathing that Narnian air. What's more, I believe this is exactly what Lewis (and God) intended.

In saying this, I'm not suggesting that the Chronicles are equivalent to Scripture, or that reading them has led me to neglect the Bible. If anything, my love for Jesus and the Book that reveals him has increased because of Lewis's efforts in the Chronicles. What I am suggesting is that I have received the same sort of grace and comfort and encouragement and motivation from Narnia as I have received from expositional preaching, small group accountability, theological tomes, and devotional writings. In short, I have been discipled as a faithful Christian through living like a Narnian. And my aim in this book is to encourage you to do the same. In other words, I want to make a case for Narnian discipleship, not merely as a coincidental byproduct of reading the Narnian stories, but as one of Lewis's (and God's!) chief goals in the Chronicles themselves.

I recognize that this is a rather bold claim, and so before proceeding to the remaining chapters, I'd like to explore what the Chronicles are. To do so, I need to say something about Lewis's understanding of fairy tales, and something about Lewis's vision of discipleship. So with that as the goal, let us return to those bubbling images.

Lewis "The Man"

Lewis writes that, as the images bubble up, the Author in him begins to long for the images to coalesce into a particular Form, whether poetry or a novel or a play. With the initial Narnian images, the Form that seemed most suitable was the fairy tale. Lewis describes his reaction to this "wedding" of Images and Form.

> The moment I thought of that I fell in love with the Form itself: its brevity, its severe restraints on description, its flexible traditionalism, its inflexible hostility to all analysis, digression, reflections and 'gas'. I was now enamoured of it.[3]

Lewis goes on to describe how "the Man" in him (his term for the part of us that evaluates whether we should do what our loves and desires are telling us to do) then began to go to work. I'll return to Lewis the Man at the end of this introduction. For the moment, let us think more carefully about the particular Form that the stories take.

ARE THEY ALLEGORIES?

Many Christian readers, upon discovering additional layers of meaning in the Narnian stories, immediately jump to the conclusion that the Chronicles are allegories. These same readers would be surprised to learn that C. S. Lewis denied multiple times that the stories are allegories. In a letter to Sophia Storr, he wrote, "But it is not, as some people think, an allegory."[4] Elsewhere, he wrote, "You are mistaken when you think that everything in the books 'represents' something in this world. Things do that in *The Pilgrim's Progress* but I'm not writing in that way."[5]

Lewis defined allegory as "a composition (whether pictorial or literary) in which immaterial realities are represented by feigned physical objects, e.g. a pictured Cupid allegorically represents erotic love (which in reality is an experience, not an object occupying a given area of space) or, in Bunyan, a giant represents Despair."[6] The two key components of this definition are:

1. allegories are imagined ("feigned") physical objects, and
2. they represent non-physical ("immaterial") realities.

In denying that the Narnian stories are allegories, Lewis does not thereby deny the Christian meaning inherent in the stories. But his goal was more nuanced than a representation of unseen reality; the literary device he chose is more aptly called "a supposal." Here's Lewis in his own words:

I did not say to myself 'Let us represent Jesus as He really is in our world by a Lion in Narnia': I said 'Let us *suppose* that there were a land like Narnia and that the Son of God, as He became a Man in our world, became a Lion there, and then imagine what would have happened.' If you think about it, you will see that it is quite a different thing.[7]

Or again,

If Aslan represented the immaterial Deity, he would be an allegorical figure. In reality however he is an invention giving an imaginary answer to the question, 'What might Christ become like if there really were a world like Narnia and He chose to be incarnate and die and rise again in that world as He actually has done in ours.'[8]

This distinction between allegory and supposal can aid us as we seek to be discipled as true Narnians. Because allegorical figures make abstract realities in our world more concrete, the action still takes place in this world. Giant Despair simply becomes a name for our own struggles in this world. The connection between the narrative world and the world we inhabit is so tight that we never truly leave our own. (These comments should not be taken as a criticism of allegories, least of all, Bunyan's masterpiece.)

In contrast, a "supposal" forces us out of our world into another one, what Lewis's friend J.R.R. Tolkien described as a "secondary world." By creating Narnia, Lewis invites us out of our own skin and into that of Peter, Susan, Edmund, and Lucy (and later Caspian, Eustace, Jill, Shasta, and the rest). The challenges we face are Narnian challenges. The victories we win are Narnian victories. But our time in Narnia is not an end in itself. We go *there* so that we then can live better *here*. By taking us out of this world, Lewis enables us to become something that we weren't before, something greater and grander, so that, when we return out of the wardrobe, we face our own Giants of Despair differently. We face them as true Narnians.

ARE FAIRY TALES SUITABLE FOR CHILDREN?

So then, the Narnian stories are "supposals," a kind of fairy tale that takes us into an imaginary world in order to shape the kind of people that we are. If this is the case, then we must face two, almost opposing, questions. First, are fairy tales, with their escapism and dragons and villains, really suitable for children? And second, if they are for children, are they *only* for children?

Lewis was aware that many regarded fairy stories as unsuitable even for children. In "On Three Ways of Writing for Children," he sets out to defend the fairy tale against three objections.

Objection 1: Fairy tales give children a false impression of the world.

On the contrary, Lewis responds, fairy stories give them a realistic impression of the world. In fact, it's the so-called "realistic" stories that are more likely to deceive them. "All stories in which children have adventures and successes which are possible, in the sense that they do not break the laws of nature, but almost infinitely improbable, are in more danger than fairy tales of raising false expectations."[9]

Objection 2: They promote escapism in children.

Lewis responds by noting that both fairy stories and realistic stories engage in "wish-fulfillment." But it is actually the realistic stories that are more deadly. Fairy stories do awaken desires in children, but most often it's not a desire for the fairy world itself. Most children don't really want there to be dragons in modern England. Instead, the desire is for "they know not what." This desire for "something beyond" does not empty the real world, but actually gives it new depths. "He does not despise real woods because he has read of enchanted woods: the reading makes all real woods a little enchanted."[10]

Realistic stories, on the other hand, are fraught with danger in that they tend to provoke resentment and anger. A child who reads about a boy who tells the truth despite difficulty at school and is acclaimed for it will most likely be disappointed when his own hard truth-telling is not met with the same accolades. Stories about realistic, but highly improbable scenarios send children back to their lives "undivinely discontented." The boy feels cheated, believing that the things in the story "would have happened if the reader had had a fair chance" (38).

Objection 3: They will frighten children.

To this objection, Lewis believes that we must carefully define what we mean by "frighten." If we mean that we must not instill "disabling, pathological fears" in children, well and good. The trouble is that we often don't know what will trigger such phobias in children (Lewis notes that his own night-terrors as a child centered on insects, something which he received from the real world and not from fairy tales).

But in making this objection, some mean that "we must try to keep out of [the child's] mind the knowledge that he is born into a world of death, violence, wounds, adventure, heroism and cowardice, good and evil." However, Lewis says, we are born into a world like that, and hiding it from children actually handicaps them. "Since it is so likely that they will meet cruel enemies, let them at least have heard of brave knights and heroic courage. . . . Let there be wicked kings and beheadings, battles and dungeons, giants and dragons, and let villains be soundly killed at the end of the book."[11]

Indeed, Lewis argues that exposing children to the second type of fear can help them to overcome the first type of debilitating phobia.

I think it is possible that by confining your child to blameless stories of child life in which nothing at all alarming ever happens, you would fail to banish the terrors and would succeed in banishing all that can ennoble them or make them endurable. For in the fairy tales, side by side with the terrible figures, we find the immemorial comforters and protectors, the radiant ones....It would be nice if no little boy in bed, hearing, or thinking he hears a sound, were ever at all frightened. But if he is going to be frightened, I think it better that he should think of giants and dragons than merely of burglars. And I think St. George, or any bright champion in armour, is a better comfort than the idea of the police.[12]

ARE FAIRY TALES *ONLY* FOR CHILDREN?

Having established that children should be allowed (and encouraged) to read fairy tales, we now ask the other pressing question, "Are such stories, with their fanciful creatures and lack of realism, only suitable for children? Shouldn't adults be above such childish things?"

Following his friend Tolkien, Lewis recognized that the association of fairy tales with children was a relatively recent and misleading phenomenon. In fact, he wrote, "I am almost inclined to set it up as a canon that a children's story which is only enjoyed by children is a bad children's story."[13] Or again, "it is certainly my opinion that a book worth reading only in childhood is not worth reading even then."[14]

In response to those who regard adult lovers of fairy tales as childish and suffering from arrested development, Lewis turns the tables and reminds us that the obsession with being "grown-up" is the mark of adolescence, not adulthood. "When I became a man I put away childish things, including the fear of childishness and the desire to be very grown up."[15] Growing up doesn't mean replacing old loves as much as it means adding new ones. Thus, a love of Aslan and Narnia ought not be limited to children, as though it were beneath adults. In fact, adults ought to be able to find *more* to love in the stories (this has certainly been my experience). Especially, if the author intends for his readers to be edified, educated, and discipled by them.

C. S. LEWIS VS. MODERN EDUCATION

We have seen that Lewis loved fairy tales and regarded them as beneficial for both children and adults. Lewis would have shared Peter Leithart's assessment of the potency of stories in shaping who we are.

> There are many mysteries in trying to unravel how reading shapes the self....Mimesis or imitation is one of the fundamental realities in the formation of the self. Children learn language, manners, gestures, parenting (!), and a host of other habits and passions from their parents, without either parents or children putting much conscious effort into it. And the dance of mimesis does not end with childhood: Disciples become like their masters, soldiers are molded by their commander, and college basketball players (and many flabby former players) aspire to 'be like Mike.' It is absurd to suggest that fictional characters, whom most readers know more intimately than they know their own parents, do not have a similar effect. Earlier critics took it for granted that literature, an imitation of life, presents models for imitation to the reader.[16]

The focus on imitation and habit formation brings us to the question of discipleship. My contention is that Lewis intends the Narnian stories to inculcate Christian beliefs, values, habits, and affections. By reflecting on Lewis's critique of modern education in his brilliant little book *The Abolition of Man*, we can better apprehend how he viewed the process of discipleship.

Lewis regarded the trends in the educational establishment of his day as problematic on a number of levels. Choosing an English textbook as his starting point, Lewis offers a shrewd and perceptive critique of the subtle ways in which our educational assumptions and models can negatively impact a society.

The Marginalization of Value Statements

First, Lewis highlights the sly ways that modern education marginalizes value statements. The authors of *The Green Book*, whom he chose as his sparring partners, state that when we make a value statement about something in the world, we are not actually speaking about the thing itself, but instead making a statement about our own subjective feelings. In other words, when we stand at the edge of the Grand Canyon and exclaim, "That is glorious!" we are not really commenting about the canyon; rather we are simply communicating that we have feelings associated in our minds with the word "glory." What's more, due to the modern quest (some might say lust) for "objectivity," statements about our subjective impressions are insignificant and easily dismissed as mere opinion with nothing of value to offer the world. Lewis writes,

> The schoolboy who reads this passage in *The Green Book* will believe two propositions: firstly, that all sentences containing a predicate of value are statements about the emotional state of the speaker, and, secondly, that all such statements are unimportant. (19)[17]

The Separation of Fact and Value

Second, this marginalization of value statements results in a sharp separation in the mind of the student between objective "facts" and subjective "values." The former are rational, testable, and important. The latter are "contrary to reason and contemptible" (25). Moreover, this separation of fact and value is not a creed that is taught explicitly, but an atmosphere and tone that is inhaled and absorbed. It is something "in the air," which becomes a part of a student's mental framework and assumptions, exerting substantial influence upon him without critical analysis or reflection.

The Creation of Men without Chests

Third, a student who thus begins to assume this fact-value distinction will begin to display two traits that are harmful to himself and to society. First, he will begin to view ordinary human emotions disdainfully. He will look down his nose at a mother who is delighted by her children or an old man who tears up when the national anthem is played. Second, this disdain of ordinary emotions will be accompanied by a decreasing practice of classical virtues like courage, sacrifice, and honor. The reason is not hard to see. Familial affection (like that between a mother and child) is the source of self-sacrifice on the part of the mother. The tears of the patriot are intimately connected to his willingness to fight for the flag.

These two factors will have devastating effects on the student and on the society. The student will have cut himself off from the possibility of "having certain experiences which thinkers of more authority than [he] have held to be generous, fruitful, and humane" (23). The society in which he lives, which has promoted and celebrated this type of modern education, will be in an ironically broken state:

And all the time—such is the tragi-comedy of our situation—we continue to clamour for those very qualities we are rendering impossible. You can hardly open a periodical without coming across the statement that what our civilization needs is more 'drive,' or dynamism, or self-sacrifice, or 'creativity.' In a sort of ghastly simplicity we remove the organ and demand the function. We make men without chests and expect of them virtue and enterprise. We laugh at honour and are shocked to find traitors in our midst. We castrate and bid the geldings be fruitful. (36–37)

In highlighting "men without chests," Lewis is not merely lamenting the loss of virtues like courage, fidelity, and sacrifice. For he knows that nature abhors a vacuum, and in the absence of these virtues, men will turn elsewhere to find meaning and purpose.

The Appeal to Instinct and the Rebellion of Branches against the Tree

Lewis rejects the notion that those who are debunking "traditional values" are themselves value-less. "A great many of those who 'debunk' traditional or (as they would say) 'sentimental' values have in the background values of their own which they believe to be immune from the debunking process" (43). Indeed, Lewis contends that these "skeptics" would be well-served to be a little more skeptical about their own system of values. For, having rejected the *Tao* (Lewis's word for the God-given order of the world and its expressions in Natural Law and Traditional Morality), these innovators simply end up elevating "Instinct" to an ultimate value.

The difficulty with obeying "Instinct" is threefold. First, Instinct is just a word for phenomena that we can't explain ("to say that migratory birds find their way by instinct is only to say that we do not know how migratory birds find their way," 46). In this sense, appeals to Instinct plant our feet firmly in mid-air. Second, "telling us to obey instinct is like telling us to obey 'people.' People say different things; so do instincts. Our instincts are at war" (49). Finally, if we dive further into this appeal to Instinct, we discover that these innovators are borrowing from Traditional Morality in order to attack Traditional Morality. As Lewis says, this "is a rebellion of the branches against the tree: if the rebels could succeed they would find that they had destroyed themselves" (56).

The Rejection of Value and the Attempt to Conquer Nature

Finally, faced with such a self-contradiction, the innovators are forced to take one more step. Rather than attempting to separate fact and value and subsequently elevate Instinct as an ultimate value, they can simply reject the concept of "value" altogether. In the place of ultimate values, they substitute what has become a near-obsession in the modern world: Man's conquest of Nature through science and technology. Space limits my ability to unpack Lewis's analysis of this phenomenon, so I will simply restate his two conclusions:

First, "Man's conquest of Nature, if the dreams of some scientific planners are realized means the rule of a few hundreds of men over billions upon billions of men" (69). The reason is simply that the attempt to conquer Nature must culminate in the conquest of *human* nature. In other words, ultimately these innovators (which Lewis dubs "Conditioners") have as their aim the refashioning of Mankind. But in order to remake Mankind, they must relinquish their stake in it, stepping outside the obligations that are derived from something above Man (namely, God) and the ties that bind men together in order to guide and condition the remaining men into whatever image they please.

Second, having stepped outside of the God-given order of the world that stands over and above all men, these Conditioners cease to be men at all (at least in the traditional sense of the word). "Man's final conquest has proved to be the abolition of Man" (74). Indeed, "At the moment, then, of Man's victory over Nature, we find the whole human race subjected to some individual men, and those individuals subjected to that in themselves which is purely 'natural'—to their irrational impulses. Nature, untrammeled by values, rules the Conditioners and, through them, all humanity. Man's conquest of Nature turns out, in the moment of its consummation, to be Nature's conquest of Man."

To summarize, Lewis sees the progression like this: 1) the marginalization of value statements leads to 2) the separation of fact from value, which leads to 3) the creation of men without chests, which leads to 4) the elevation of "instinct" as an ultimate value, which, because of its own self-contradictions, leads to 5) man's attempt to conquer nature through science and technology and 6) the tyranny of the conditioners over mankind, which in the end is 7) the abolition of man.

Such is the trajectory of modern education, and it is a trajectory that Lewis is committed to reversing. His means? An older—and better—view of man and education.

LEWIS'S ALTERNATIVE VIEW OF EDUCATION

Having examined the form of education that Lewis rejects, we turn now to a brief summation of his own view. The following tenets are not the whole of Lewis's educational paradigm, but instead form some of the non-negotiables that Lewis felt were under particular attack in his day.

The Tao

Genuine education embraces the *Tao*, the term Lewis adopts for the God-given order in the world. For Lewis, the *Tao* is a combination of the absoluteness of reality and the human way of life that conforms to this reality. In other words, reality simply is a certain way, and human beings are called to order their lives by the pattern of the *Tao*. Lewis identifies the *Tao* as Natural Law, Traditional Morality, and First Principles. He believed that some aspect of the *Tao* was present in all major ancient philosophies and religions (Christian, Platonic, Oriental, Stoic, etc). Biblical support for such an idea may be found in Romans 1, where what can be known about God (i.e., Absolute Reality) has been revealed to and perceived by all men because God has made it known, so that men are without excuse.

The Doctrine of Objective Value

For Lewis, the common feature in all manifestations of the *Tao* is the doctrine of objective value:

> Until quite modern times all teachers and even all men believed the universe to be such that certain emotional reactions on our part could be either congruous or incongruous to it—believed, in fact, that objects did not merely receive, but could *merit* our approval or disapproval, our reverence, or our contempt. (27–28)

> It is the doctrine of objective value, the belief that certain attitudes are really true, and others really false, to the kind of thing the universe is and the kind of things we are. Those who know the *Tao* can hold that to call children delightful or old men venerable is not simply to record a psychological fact about our own parental or filial emotions at the moment, but to recognize a quality which *demands* a certain response from us whether we make it or not. (31)

In short, the "givenness" of the world—and in particular, the Ultimate Reality that stands behind it—means that when we are confronted with various aspects of reality, we are obligated to respond with certain rational and emotional reactions. What's more, the doctrine of objective value is absolutely essential for human flourishing, both as individuals and in societies. "Only the *Tao* provides a common human law of action which can overarch rulers and ruled alike. A dogmatic belief in objective value is necessary to the very idea of a rule which is not tyranny or an obedience which is not slavery" (81).

The Principle of Proportionate Regard

But it's not enough to simply feel *something* in response to the objective reality of the world. You must also feel rightly and *proportionately* to the way the world is.

> "Can you be righteous," asks Traherne, "unless you be just in rendering to things their due esteem? All things were made to be yours and you were made to prize them according to their value?"…St. Augustine defines virtue as *ordo amoris*, the ordinate condition of the affections in which every object is accorded that kind and degree of love which is appropriate to it. Aristotle says that the aim of education is to make the pupil like and dislike what he ought. (28–29)

These three realities form the foundation of true education. They also shape the aim of education.

> For those within [the *Tao*], the task is to train in the pupil those responses which are themselves appropriate…. (32)

> The little human animal will not at first have the right responses. It must be trained to feel pleasure, liking, disgust, and hatred at those things which really are pleasant, likeable, disgusting, and hateful. (32)

Following Plato, Lewis believed that we ought to initiate the young into these right responses, even before they are able to rationally understand or explain what they are feeling. The goal of such inculcation of right responses is that, when a child raised in this way grows up and encounters Truth, Goodness, and Beauty, he will welcome them with open arms, because he has been prepared for, and indeed, resembles them already.

Which brings us, finally, to the function of the Narnian stories in Lewis's vision of education. The Narnian stories display through imaginative fiction and fairy tale *the way that the world really is.*

Here is courage and bravery in its shining glory. Here is honesty and truth-telling in its simplicity and profundity. Here is treachery in all its ugliness. Here is the face of Evil. Here also is the face of Good. A child (or adult) who lives in such stories will have developed the patterns of thought and affection that will be well-prepared to embrace the True, the Good, and the Beautiful (that is, to embrace Jesus Christ) when he finally encounters them (Him!). Like John the Baptist, Lewis and his cast of Narnians will have prepared the way.

BACK TO THE BUBBLING

It is this vision of education and discipleship that Lewis the Man brought to bear when he considered the images of a faun, a witch, and a lion that were bubbling into a fairy tale. He began to recognize the potency that such stories might have for his readers.

> I thought I saw how stories of this kind could steal past a certain inhibition which paralyzed much of my own religion since childhood. Why did one find it so hard to feel as one was told one ought to feel about God or about the sufferings of Christ? I thought the chief reason was that one was told one ought to. An obligation can freeze feelings. And reverence itself did harm. The whole subject was associated with lowered voices; almost as if it were something medical. But suppose casting all these things into an imaginary world, stripping them of their stained-glass and Sunday school associations, one could make them for the first time appear in their real potency? Could one not thus steal past the watchful dragons? I thought one could.[18]

This paragraph can give us great insight in how we ought to read the Narnian stories. We ought not begin by trying to identify every Christian correspondence or layer of meaning. We must not short-circuit the shaping process. Instead (and this is especially important when introducing children to the stories) we ought to first immerse ourselves in the stories *as stories*. We must learn to trek across the Narnian countryside, swim in the Narnian seas, distinguish Calormenes from Archenlanders, and navigate the etiquette of centaurs (it's a very serious thing to invite a centaur to dinner; they have two stomachs after all). Indeed, we must learn to breathe Narnian air, a metaphor that Lewis uses elsewhere to describe what it means to come to know God. Then, having learned our Narnian stars and feasted at Cair Paravel—in other words, once we've stolen past the watchful dragons—we can then turn our attention to the deeper, Christian layers of meaning, the textures of the story that have bubbled up from Lewis's mind.

Indeed, as Aslan says to Lucy on one occasion, "This was the very reason you were brought into Narnia, that by knowing me here for a little, you might know me better there."

1

Deep Magic, and Deeper

The Moral Law and Sacrificial Love

The presence of magic in the Chronicles has been cause for concern among some Christian parents. They wonder whether exposing young children to stories containing magic will awaken a desire in them to pursue something that the Bible has forbidden. For some parents, this concern rises to the level of a conviction, and they shield their kids from any fiction (including the Chronicles) that portrays magic in a positive light. Even parents who don't forbid the Chronicles may wonder how to think rightly and biblically about the presence of magic throughout Lewis's stories. The aim of this chapter is to provide a brief overview of what the Bible says about magic and then a quick look at Lewis's use of magic in *The Lion, the Witch, and the Wardrobe*.

First, the Bible teaches that magic is real. Simon the Magician amazed the people of Samaria with his magic (Acts 8:9–11). In Isaiah, God acknowledges "the great power" of the enchantments of the sorcerers of Egypt (47:9). The Egyptian sorcerers are able to duplicate the signs and wonders of Moses and Aaron by "their secret arts": staffs into serpents (Ex. 7:11–12), the Nile into blood

(7:22), and the plague of frogs (8:7). So we ought not think of all magic as simply sleight of hand or eye-tricking illusions. Magic is a real feature of the world that God has made.

Second, the Bible forbids sorcery, fortune-telling, divination, and the interpretation of omens (Ex. 22:18; Deut. 18:10). Such witchcraft is often linked to other sins: idolatry (2 Kings 9:22; Rev. 21:8), sexual immorality (Mal. 3:5), and child-sacrifice (2 Chron. 33:6). The Bible is clear that those who practice such things will not inherit the kingdom of God (Gal. 5:19–21; Rev. 21:8; 22:15).

Third, despite these prohibitions, faithful believers are numbered among the magicians in Gentile courts. Joseph is called to interpret Pharaoh's dreams when his own magicians fail (Gen. 41:8, 14–36). Daniel and his three friends are numbered among the magicians and enchanters of Babylon (Dan. 1:20). Indeed, Daniel is the "chief of the magicians" (Dan. 4:9, 5:11). Of course, both Joseph and Daniel are successful as wise men and magicians because God reveals to them the interpretation of dreams and gives them wisdom and understanding (Gen. 41:16; Dan. 2:28–30). In addition to these men, the magi who bring gifts to baby Jesus do so because of their astrological efforts in following the star of Bethlehem (Matt. 2:1–12). The Semitic root *magi* is where we get our English word *magic*.

Beyond this, if we adopt the standard dictionary definition of magic as "the power of apparently influencing the course of events by using mysterious or supernatural forces," then we might think of miracles and signs and wonders as a kind of "magic." The magical combat between Moses and the magicians of Egypt would indicate as much. A similar power encounter occurs in Acts 13. Elymas the magician is a Jewish false prophet who opposed the apostles and sought to turn people away from the faith (Acts 13:6–8). Paul, filled with Holy Spirit, calls down the power of God on that "son of the devil" and "enemy of all righteousness," inflicting him with blindness (13:9–11). The difference between the dark magic of the Egyptian magicians and Elymas on the one hand, and Moses and Paul on the other was not *what* they were doing, but the source of their power. Indeed, what distinguishes sorcery, witchcraft, and black magic from godly miracles, signs, and "white magic" is the source of power (God or demons) and the purpose of the power (worshiping the true God and serving people, or worshiping idols and dominating people). Thus, the Bible is filled with stories of prophets and men of God doing what can best be described as magic: magic bread from heaven, floating ax heads, walking on water, restoring sight using spit and mud, handkerchiefs that heal sickness, a virgin birth, and resurrection from the dead.

Narnian Magic

So then, according to the Bible, the power of influencing the world using supernatural forces (i.e., magic) is very real. When used to lead people into idolatry and sin or to oppress and enslave others, it is forbidden. On the other hand, when we acknowledge we ultimately do not control God and his power, and we seek power from the hand of God for the good of people, God's miraculous signs and wonders through us might be described as a kind of good magic.

When we come to *The Lion, the Witch, and the Wardrobe*, we see Lewis operating within these biblical categories. Black magic is certainly on display in the Witch's enchantment of Narnia: "She has made a magic so that it is always winter in Narnia—always winter but it never gets to Christmas" (Ch. 4). The Witch conjures enchanted and addicting Turkish Delight from a small bottle, and with her wand she is able to turn people into stone statues.

At the same time, there is a kind of white magic in the stories: a magic wardrobe that is a doorway to another world as well as a "magic" in the house that came to life and chased the children into Narnia (Ch. 5). Such magic is mysterious and beyond the children's ability to control; they're unable to enter Narnia at will.

Beyond this general magic, there is Aslan's enchantment-breaking magic: When Aslan is on the move, the Witch's magic weakens and Father Christmas is able to enter Narnia (Ch. 10). Aslan's arrival brings an end to the Witch's enslaving spell and the happy onset of spring. Aslan restores the stone statues to life through his powerful, life-giving breath.

So in Narnia, as in the real world, there is black magic, which enslaves and oppresses people, as well as white magic, which liberates and restores people. Black magic is power over others for the purpose of harm. White magic is power under divine authority for the good of others. But there are yet other forms of magic in Narnia, which Lewis employs to teach us something profound about our own world.

Deep Magic Triumphs

After Aslan's army rescues Edmund from the White Witch, the Witch approaches Aslan and identifies Edmund as a traitor, who lawfully belongs to the Witch and can be put to death for his treachery (Ch. 13). She bases her claim on the Deep Magic, a Magic that is written on the Stone Table and "engraved on the scepter of the Emperor-beyond-the-Sea," a Magic that the Emperor placed in Narnia at the very beginning. Deep Magic is the Law of the Emperor, the expression of his character, and upholding it is essential for the existence and integrity of Narnia. The very suggestion that Aslan work against the Emperor's Magic is met with a shock and a disapproving frown, so that "nobody ever made that suggestion to him again."

For Lewis, the Deep Magic is the Moral Law—what in *The Abolition of Man* he calls the *Tao*—the fundamental moral framework upon which the universe is based. It is a reflection of God's own harmonious order, the walls around the City that make life inside possible. As G. K. Chesterton reminded us, the reason that order and structure exist in the world is so that good things can run wild.

But, in this case (to modify the apostle Paul), the Deep Magic that promised life proved to be death for Edmund. Or, at least, it appeared that way. But while Aslan will not work against the Emperor's Magic, all is not lost for the doomed young boy. Aslan shows a better, and more difficult, way. For though the Deep Magic does demand blood for treachery, it also allows substitutes, and Aslan willingly gives himself for Edmund so that the Witch renounces her claim on the boy and kills Aslan in his place. Thus, Deep Magic is satisfied.

But even this Deep Magic doesn't exhaust Lewis's vision of the world. There is a Deeper Magic still, and it rises with the dawn on the morning after Aslan's sacrifice. The Stone Table breaks in two and Aslan's body is gone. Confused, Susan cries out,

> "What does it mean? Is it more magic?"
>
> "Yes!" said a great voice behind their backs. "It is more magic."
>
> "It means," said Aslan, "that though the Witch knew the Deep Magic, there is a magic deeper still which she did not know. Her knowledge goes back only to the dawn of time. But if she could have looked a little further back, into the stillness and the darkness before Time dawned, she would have read there a different incantation. She would have known that when a willing victim who had committed no treachery was killed in a traitor's stead, the Table would crack and Death itself would start working backward." (Ch. 15)

This is the true picture of magic in Narnia, and it's magic is mirrored in our own world. Conflicts of power and enchantments are real, and they matter. But beneath the power encounters and magical warfare is Deep Magic and Deeper, the inflexible solidity of the Moral Law and the breath-taking beauty of Sacrificial Love. Lewis reminds us that substitution is a kind of magic, a mysterious and supernatural force that transforms the world, overcoming every form of treachery. In Narnia, as in our world, Deeper Magic triumphs over Deep Magic. Through sacrifice, Mercy triumphs over Judgment.

2

The Witch's War on Joy

*Why Christmas, Feasts, and Spring's Arrival
Really Matter*

As a transplant to Minnesota from Texas, one of the things I'm
fond of saying is that Minnesota in February is a land that only the
White Witch could love: it's always winter and never Christmas.
And the comparison goes beyond the sheer fact of the winter. February gets all of the holidays that none of the other months wanted:
Presidents Day, Groundhog Day (a holiday whose only saving grace
is Bill Murray's classic comedy), and Valentine's Day, which, as
Charlie Brown might say, is a commercial racket run by an Eastern
syndicate. March has Spring Break and St. Patrick's Day. April has
Easter. May has Mother's Day and Memorial Day. June is essentially
one long holiday, and so on.

It's the combination of frigid bleakness and the absence of true
festivity that makes February so depressing. And this is precisely
the Witch's mark: winter without expectation of joy, winter without
Christmas.

What Spring Brings

The contrast between the Witch and Aslan at this point is one of
the central themes of the first Narnian book. A key scene occurs in
Chapter 11 when the Witch and Edmund are traveling through the
woods in pursuit of the beavers and the other children. They happen upon "a merry party" made up of a squirrel family, two satyrs, a
fox, and a Dwarf, seated at a table and enjoying a delicious holiday
meal. The Witch is incensed and demands to know, "What is the
meaning of all this gluttony, this waste, this self-indulgence?" When
she discovers that the meal was a gift from Father Christmas, she
turns the entire party into stone.

The benefit of the scene is that it demonstrates that the Witch's
evil is not fundamentally about winter and cold weather, but about
a deep-seated hostility to life, joy, and celebration. The Witch loves
death, and her icy curse on Narnia is simply one expression of this
overall hatred of life. Indeed, the accent is not on winter itself, but
the fact that it is *always* winter and *never* Christmas. Winter has a
crucial place in the yearly cycle of renewal and the turning of the
seasons. But winter should be inhabited by holiday celebration
and should ultimately be propelling us forward to spring, and it's
precisely this forward-looking expectation and celebratory "jollification" that the Witch opposes with all her dark arts.

The contrast with Aslan couldn't be starker. I've already mentioned Father Christmas, who was kept out of Narnia by the Witch,
but is finally allowed in with his gifts and festivity thanks to Aslan's
arrival. When Aslan himself lands in Narnia, we are treated to a
lengthy and detailed description of his effects on nature: the melting of snow, the unthawing of rivers, the appearance of flowers and
green grass, the shining of delicious sunlight, the wafting of lovely
smells, and the chirping of birds in the trees. Despite their overall
ignorance of Narnia, the children are aware "that it was her spells
which had produced the endless winter; and therefore they all knew
when this magic spring began that something had gone wrong,

and badly wrong, with the Witch's schemes" (Ch. 12). The Witch's Dwarf is more explicit: "This is no thaw. . . . This is *Spring*. What are we to do? Your winter has been destroyed, I tell you! This is Aslan's doing" (Ch. 11).

The Importance of Food

But again the contrast goes beyond the weather and seasonal change, and perhaps surprisingly, centers in key ways on food. The Witch expresses anger at gluttony and self-indulgence; however, she also gives Edmund Turkish Delight that has been enchanted so that "anyone who had once tasted it would want more and more of it, and would even, if they were allowed, go on eating it till they killed themselves" (Ch. 4). Indeed, the Witch provides two meals to Edmund: the enchanted candy and stale bread and water. The Witch and her evil are the origins of both gluttony and asceticism, of sinful indulgence and sinful austerity.

Aslan, however, is another story. After he first meets Peter, Susan, and Lucy, he immediately commands, "Let the feast be prepared." After the final battle with the Witch, Aslan provides a fine high tea for his army. And, of course, the night that the four children are enthroned, "there was a great feast in Cair Paravel, and revelry and dancing, and gold flashed and wine flowed" (Ch. 17).

But it's not only Aslan who provides delightful meals for his people. The Faun Tumnus, despite his ulterior motives, initially provides Lucy with a fine tea with eggs, sardines, buttered toast, honey, and cake. Meanwhile, he regales her with stories about the time before the Witch:

> He told about the midnight dances and how the Nymphs who lived in the wells and the Dryads who lived in the trees came out to dance with the Fauns; about long hunting parties after the milk-white stag who could give you wishes if you caught him; about feasting and treasure-seeking with the wild Red Dwarfs in deep mines and caverns far

beneath the forest floor; and then about summer when the woods were green and old Silenus on his fat donkey would come to visit them, and sometimes Bacchus himself, and then the streams would run with wine instead of water and the whole forest would give itself up to jollification for weeks on end. (Ch. 2)

And lest we think that the point is perpetual feasts and lavish displays of indulgence, the beavers provide the children with a simple meal of fresh fish, buttered potatoes, creamy milk, and a marmalade roll. Afterwards, they all lean against the wall and give "a long sigh of contentment" (Ch. 7). The size or expense of the meal isn't the point; the attitude and receptivity of the meal is.

Making Merry Like It Matters

I can't speak for everyone, but breathing this type of Narnian air has a particular effect on me, one that I think Lewis intended. For starters, Lewis's descriptions of food tend to make me hungry (though having tried Turkish Delight, I fail to see the appeal; the fact that Edmund requests it is for me a sign that he's already on his way to the Witch's side).

But more than just awakening my hunger, breathing Narnian air awakens a desire for a particular type of meal, one with tasty food, good conversation, lots of joy and laughter and revelry and strategizing about how to defeat the White Witch.

It makes me want to eat my bread with joy and drink my wine with a merry heart, because God approves (Eccles. 9:7). It makes me want to guard my heart against gluttony *and* miserliness. It makes me want to live so that those with shriveled hearts and icy minds accuse me of self-indulgence and waste. It also makes me want to live so that the accusations are false.

It makes me want to pay attention at mealtimes, both to the food on my plate and the friends at the table. It makes me want to enjoy high feasts on appropriate occasions, to eat simple meals as though they mattered (because they do), and to teach my children by example the meaning of jollification (hint: dancing is required).

And the glorious truth is that Lewis's vision of feasting through winter and glorying in spring and resisting the seductive dullness of the Witch's world is not just a fairy tale, but the way the world *really* is. In the bleak mid-winter long ago, Spring landed in Bethlehem and began to unthaw the world. Frozen rivers melted and stone statues began to come to life. The Son of Man came eating and drinking and magically turning water into wine and multiplying loaves and fishes on a grassy hillside. Accused of gluttony and indulgence, he endured the scorn and violence of men with ice in their veins. Dying for those who feasted on the Witch's food, he broke his own Stone Table and is now casting out the wicked and arrogant so that the meek can inherit the earth and sit on thrones at a great wedding supper. Because Jesus, like Aslan, is Lord of the Feast.

3

We Will Be Who We Are Becoming

Our Direction Determines Our Destination

A recurring theme in all of the Narnian books is the relationship between our character and our actions, between the type of person that we are and the way that we respond to our circumstances. Put simply, who you are determines what you hear, how you think, how you respond to temptation and failure, how you react to unpleasant situations, and how you respond to beauty and glory. Or to put it in more biblical terms, out of the overflow of the heart the mouth speaks, and the mind thinks, and the heart feels.

Edmund in Our World

In *The Lion, the Witch, and the Wardrobe*, Edmund is a perfect example of this truth. When we first meet Edmund, he's tired and bad-tempered, resisting his older sister's encouragement to go to bed. "Who are you to say when I'm to go to bed? Go to bed yourself" (Ch. 1). Later, after Lucy returns from Narnia and the others don't believe her, we're told that "Edmund could be spiteful," and that he "sneered and jeered at Lucy." When he sees her entering the wardrobe, he follows her "because he wanted to go on teasing her about her imaginary country" (Ch. 3).

Entering Narnia and realizing that Lucy is right, he yells out an apology to Lucy (who is nowhere to be found), and when she doesn't respond, Edmund shows his lack of sincerity by saying, "Just like a girl. . . . sulking somewhere and won't accept an apology." When he finally does meet her, he again provides a perfect example of how *not* to apologize: "All right, I see you were right and it is a magic wardrobe after all. I'll say I'm sorry if you like" (Ch. 4). In both cases, his apology is not driven by genuine remorse, but by a thin sense of obligation and a desire to save face. Edmund, we come to see, only seeks forgiveness and reconciliation grudgingly.

Later, after the two return from Narnia, Edmund does "one of the nastiest things in this story."

> And now we come to one of the nastiest things in this story. Up to that moment Edmund had been feeling sick, and sulky, and annoyed with Lucy for being right, but he hadn't made up his mind what to do. When Peter suddenly asked him the question he decided all at once to do the meanest and most spiteful thing he could think of. He decided to let Lucy down. (Ch. 5)

Putting on a very superior look, he tells Peter and Susan that he and Lucy were just playing and pretending that there was a country in the wardrobe. Lucy runs away, and Edmund suffers Peter's anger for his spitefulness to his younger sister. In the process, Peter says, "You've always liked being beastly to anyone smaller than yourself; we've seen that at school before now." Later, we're told that Edmund had started to go wrong during his first term at the horrid school he attends (Ch. 17).

Such is the type of person that Edmund is on this side of the wardrobe: spiteful, disrespectful to his older siblings, beastly to younger children, and insincere in his apologies. What then will Narnia do with a person like Edmund?

Narnia's Effect on a Beastly Boy

On his first trip into Narnia, Edmund encounters the White Witch who initially threatens to harm him, but then invites him to sit with her in her sledge so that she can question him. Edmund has no choice but to obey, and once in the sledge he eats the enchanted Turkish Delight, comes under the Witch's spell, and tells her everything she wants to know. His addiction to the enchanted food makes him lose the proper sense of fear that he'd had at first, and later it causes him to repeat the Witch's lie about Fauns. Edmund, we're told, "was already more than half on the side of the Witch" (Ch. 4). Succumbing to temptation creates an allegiance to the Witch.

At this point, someone might say, "Can we really blame Edmund? I mean, what alternative did he really have? What would have happened if Peter had been the one to meet the Witch alone in the woods? What could he have done differently under the circumstances?"

The first thing to note is that Lewis does directly address this sort of question elsewhere in the books. In *Prince Caspian*, when Lucy asks whether she is to know what would have happened if she had made a different choice, Aslan replies, "To know what would have happened, child?... said Aslan. No. Nobody is ever told that" (*Prince Caspian*, Ch. 10; repeated in *The Voyage of the Dawn Treader*, Ch. 10).

So any attempt to think about what might have been is pure speculation. But I wonder if we can see Lewis's guiding hand in the fact that it's Edmund who meets the Witch and not Peter or Lucy. Could it be that Edmund meets her precisely because he's already on the wrong path? Might we not recognize the providential will of the author in guiding a particular character to endure a particular temptation? And might this Narnian providence give us a window into the invisible hand and plan that guides our own lives?

Returning to Edmund, we've seen the seeds of wickedness in his heart on our side of the wardrobe. We see him ensnared by the enchantment of the White Witch. From there, it's all down hill. When all of the children finally get into Narnia, Edmund slips and betrays the fact that he's been there before. The others have nothing to say to him, but Edmund sulks along, saying to himself, "I'll pay you all out for this, you pack of stuck-up, self-satisfied prigs" (Ch. 6). Again, he shows no remorse for lying and being beastly to Lucy, but only a deepening bitterness at his siblings, and especially Peter. The evil in his heart is spreading and deepening and hardening.

This type of evil doesn't simply deepen in the heart; it affects the mind as well. When the children encounter the robin that leads them to Mr. Beaver, Edmund repeatedly asks how they can *know* which side the animals are on (despite robins being good birds in all the good stories (Chs. 6, 7). Having come under the sway of the Witch, Edmund's thought processes are now warped and distorted. Incidentally, Lewis's dramatization of the intellectual effects of sin and rebellion is worth keeping in mind whenever we encounter incessant doubts and "rational" objections to Christ, either in ourselves or in others; as Paul notes in Romans 1:18–23, the futility of natural man's thinking is rooted in our ingratitude and rebellion. In Edmund's case, his supposed "intellectual objections" are merely a cover for his underlying allegiance to the Witch.

Recoiling at the Name of Aslan

The true revelation of Edmund's allegiance to the Witch comes at the first mention of Aslan in the entire series.

Here the Beaver's voice sank into silence and it gave one or two very mysterious nods. Then signaling to the children to stand as close around it as they possibly could, so that their faces were actually tickled by its whiskers, it added in a low whisper—

"They say Aslan is on the move—perhaps has already landed."

And now a very curious thing happened. None of the children knew who Aslan was any more than you do; but the moment the Beaver had spoken these words everyone felt quite different. Perhaps it has sometimes happened to you in a dream that someone says something which you don't understand but in the dream it feels as if it had some enormous meaning—either a terrifying one which turns the whole dream into a nightmare or else a lovely meaning too lovely to put into words, which makes the dream so beautiful that you remember it all your life and are always wishing you could get into that dream again. It was like that now. At the name of Aslan each one of the children felt something jump in its inside. Edmund felt a sensation of mysterious horror. Peter felt suddenly brave and adventurous. Susan felt as if some delicious smell or some delightful strain of music had just floated by her. And Lucy got the feeling you have when you wake up in the morning and realize that it is the beginning of the holidays or the beginning of summer. (Ch. 7; see the repetition of this moment in Ch. 8)

Three of the children respond to the name of Aslan by leaning in. It awakens bravery and delight and freedom in them and makes them long to see Aslan (even if they are a bit frightened as well). But Edmund has a decisively different reaction. He recoils, "For the mention of Aslan gave him a mysterious and horrible feeling just as it gave the others a mysterious and lovely feeling" (Ch. 9). His reaction to Aslan is so strong that he slips out into the cold and heads for the White Witch's house. So deep is he under the Witch's spell, that he even manages to believe (or pretend to believe) that the Witch wasn't so bad and that half of the nasty things said about her probably aren't true, demonstrating again the mind-altering and reason-deadening effects of sin and unbelief.

As he trudges through the cold and snow, his heart grows colder and harder as well. He puffs himself up about his future rule as King of Narnia. The malice in his heart grows so strong that he plots against the beavers who had only showed him kindness. And most of all, he concocts "schemes for keeping Peter in his place." And the more miserable and cold he becomes, the more he thinks about "how he hated Peter—just as if all this had been Peter's fault" (Ch. 9).

Of course, it eventually gets much worse for Edmund, as he again meets the White Witch, who is no longer pretending to be kind and friendly, and he is made to eat stale bread and water, slapped across his face, and forced to trudge through the melting snow with his hands tied behind his back. The entire experience is repeatedly described as "miserable," and culminates with the Witch sharpening a knife and preparing to kill Edmund in a sacrificial execution.

Edmund's Life As a Cautionary Tale

Edmund thus stands as a warning, a cautionary tale to everyone who reads the book. We are always becoming who we will be. We are, all of us, en-storied creatures, living our lives in a narrative, which means our lives have directions, trends, and trajectories. And these trajectories are guided by an Author who teaches us that we will reap what we sow. Right this minute, we are headed some-where, and sooner or later, we are bound to end up there. Edmund shows us that we might not like the destination at the end of our road. Indeed, it could very well be the death of us.

So we ought to ask ourselves some probing questions: Where am I compromising? Am I nursing small grievances, the kind that grow and fester into hatred of those closest to me? Do I treat those around me with respect and kindness, or do I love to show off my own perceived superiority? When I wrong someone, do I repent thoroughly, seek forgiveness sincerely, make restitution quickly, and then move on properly? Given the present trajectory of my life, what would happen if I should find myself stumbling through the wardrobe into Narnia? Will Providence guide me to meet a faun who becomes a friend, or a Witch who seeks to steal, kill, and destroy (or freeze, enchant, and murder)? Given the kind of person that I am right now becoming, what would be my reaction if I heard Aslan's name for the first time?

꙳

Post-Script

I intentionally left Edmund tied to a tree as a sacrificial victim because I think it's important to see the trajectory of his story. His whining, fussing, bullying, nastiness, and spite at the beginning of the story led him down the slippery slope of foolishness, hatred, betrayal, misery, and (almost) death. But, mercifully, Narnia is not a moral tragedy (and for that matter, neither is our world). Narnia is what Peter Leithart calls "Deep Comedy," a story in which the characters may face challenges, but eventually rise to a greater degree of glory and joy than when they began.[19]

And so, Edmund is saved from the Witch's knife and reunited with his siblings. More importantly, he meets Aslan, who forgives and restores Edmund, and then, wonder of wonders, sacrifices himself so that Edmund can be fully and completely free. Aslan's influence on Edmund is profound, as Edmund becomes wise, brave, and sacrificial in battle, breaking the Witch's wand at the cost of a terrible wound. Lucy's healing cordial restores him, not only in body, but in spirit, as he becomes "his real old self again" (Ch. 17). Once enthroned as king, he became a grave and quiet man, great in council and judgment, and was called "King Edmund the Just." And, to point ahead to Edmund's new trajectory, it's worth paying attention to his attitude and conduct in future books: the way he treats Lucy and Peter in *Prince Caspian*, the way he interacts with

Caspian and Eustace in *The Voyage of the Dawn Treader*, and the type of leader and king he is in *The Horse and His Boy*.

For now, it's enough to say that Edmund's story might have ended badly. He could have very well suffered the consequences of his actions. But Aslan, like Jesus, is full of grace, and he reaps what Edmund had sown. Mercy triumphs over Judgment, Life triumphs over Death, and for Edmund (and all those who, like him, are found by Aslan in their darkest pit) all shall be well, and all shall be well, and all manner of thing shall be well.

4

Trumpkin's Surprising Obedience

The Difference between Giving Advice and Taking Orders

Trumpkin is one of my favorite Narnians. The development of his character in *Prince Caspian* provides a central lesson in learning to live like a Narnian. However, to understand Trumpkin, we must set him over against his two friends, Trufflehunter and Nikabrik. For Lewis intends these three friends to be foils for each other, characters who shed light on each other through important comparisons and contrasts.

Contrasting the Badger and the Black Dwarf

We begin with Trufflehunter the badger. Being "the oldest and kindest of the three," he offers Caspian a drink after his fall off the horse and defends him against Nikabrik's desire to kill him. Hearing Caspian's story, he immediately embraces Caspian as the rightful king of Narnia, expressing his belief that "Narnia was never right except when a son of Adam was King" (Ch. 5). As a beast, he has a long memory and doesn't change the way humans and Dwarfs do. Thus, he both believes in the High King Peter as well as Aslan and the other Old Stories.

Nikabrik, on the other hand, is a "sour Black Dwarf." His first instinct after the three friends have brought Caspian into their home is to kill him or make him a slave. He is eaten up by hate, despising both humans and renegade Dwarfs like Dr. Cornelius. Trufflehunter's embrace of Caspian as King of Narnia makes him sick.

As the story progresses, the contrast between the two becomes even more clear. Nikabrik operates according to a mercenary logic that says "the enemy of my enemy is my friend." Thus, like the other Black Dwarfs, he eventually embraces Caspian but only because he's opposed to the evil king Miraz. Like the badger, he does believe in the Old Things, but his faith is only a means to gratify his lust for revenge. "I'll believe in anyone or anything," says Nikabrik, "that'll batter these cursed Telmarine barbarians to pieces or drive them out of Narnia. Anyone or anything, Aslan or the White Witch, do you understand?" (Ch. 6).

His willingness to embrace any and all creatures is proven when the other Black Dwarfs offer to invite some Ogres and Hags into the company. Nikabrik favors this invitation, but Trufflehunter objects to welcoming such evil creatures on the grounds that "We should not have Aslan for a friend if we brought in that rabble" (Ch. 6). Unlike Nikabrik, Trufflehunter holds true to what's True and Right in the Ancient Stories.

Trufflehunter's faith is tested when Caspian blows the magic horn and help does not arrive immediately. However, he never abandons hope. "The help will come," says Trufflehunter. "I stand by Aslan. Have patience, like us beasts. The help will come. It may be even now at the door" (Ch. 12). Nikabrik mocks Trufflehunter's faith, saying, "You badgers would have us wait till the sky falls and we can all catch larks." When Trufflehunter reminds him of his sworn allegiance to Caspian as King, Nikabrik dismisses his oath as a meaningless formality, attributing it to "court manners," as opposed to sincere loyalty.

What's more, Nikabrik again proves his pragmatic willingness to embrace anyone that will help the Old Narnians defeat the Telmarines. He invites a Hag and Werewolf into the council with the intention of calling up the White Witch. "We want power," he says, "and we want a power that will be on our side." He even falsely retells the Old Stories, speculating that Aslan never rose from the dead after being killed by the Witch. He cares little that the Witch was harsh and oppressive to humans or beasts; he's looking out for himself and the other Dwarfs. After all, the Witch "got on all right with us Dwarfs" (Ch. 12).

His lust for revenge gets the best of him, leading to his death in the fight with Caspian, Peter, and the rest. As Caspian says, "He had gone sour from long suffering and hating" (Ch. 12). On the other hand, Trufflehunter never doubts all the way through, receiving a commendation from Peter and knighthood from Caspian.

Understanding Trumpkin

The differences between Trufflehunter and Nikabrik help us better understand Trumpkin the Red Dwarf. For Trumpkin shares similarities with each of them, and yet differs from both of them in profound ways. Like Nikabrik, he was open to killing Caspian initially, but once they bandaged him up, to kill him would be unacceptable, he contends, since it would be "murdering a guest." He then defends Caspian against Nikabrik's rage and comes to trust him because Caspian "doesn't look like a traitor." His behavior thus puts him closer to Trufflehunter; however, he has a very different attitude toward the Old Stories, doubting the existence of the High King Peter, mocking belief in Naiads and Dryads, and dismissing the magical mound known as Aslan's How as an "old wives' tale."

From the beginning his attitude toward Aslan is one of disbelief and dismissal. "Who believes in Aslan nowadays?" he wonders out loud (Ch. 5). Inviting Hags and Ogres to join the Old Narnians is certainly unacceptable to Trumpkin, but not because of Aslan's disapproval. "Oh, Aslan!" says Trumpkin, cheerily but contemptuously. "What matters much more is that you wouldn't have me" (Ch. 6). Even after meeting the Kings and Queens from the ancient past, he's still lukewarm about Aslan.

> I have no use for magic lions which are talking lions and don't talk, and friendly lions though they don't do us any good, and whopping big lions though nobody can see them. It's all bilge and beanstalks as far as I can see." (Ch. 11)

Despite his profound and prolonged unbelief, the key to Trumpkin's character is found in a crucial conversation in Ch. 7. Caspian and his counselors are discussing whether to blow the magic horn to call for help. True to form, Trumpkin's attitude toward the whole question is dismissive.

> "Oh, as for me," said the Red Dwarf, who had been listening with complete indifference, "your Majesty knows I think the Horn—and that bit of broken stone over there—and your great King Peter—and your Lion Aslan—are all eggs in moonshine. It's all one to me when your Majesty blows the Horn. All I insist on is that the army is told nothing about it. There's no good raising hopes of magical help which (as I think) are sure to be disappointed."

When he hears that blowing the horn will also require sending messengers to the Ancient Places of Narnia to wait for the help, he's even more contemptuous, since the magical foolery will lose the army two fighters. Then he does something remarkable and totally unexpected. He volunteers to be one of the messengers.

> "Send me, Sire, I'll go."
> "But I thought you didn't believe in the Horn, Trumpkin," said Caspian.
> "No more I do, your Majesty. But what's that got to do with it? I

might as well die on a wild goose chase as die here. You are my King.
I know the difference between giving advice and taking orders. You've
had my advice, and now it's the time for orders."

This is the central lesson of Trumpkin: embracing obedience to
lawful authority, even when you disagree with the orders. Trumpkin may not believe in Aslan, but he's following in the ways of Aslan
just the same. His honor, his allegiance to his friends, his humility
and willingness to be taught, and his stubborn loyalty against all
odds: all of these lead to the moment when he too sees Aslan for
the first time and is welcomed by the Great Lion as a friend.

Obedience: The Great Eye-Opener

Trumpkin shows us that coming to faith is not always like getting
knocked off your horse by a blinding light. Sometimes it's a slow
process filled with unexpected twists and turns. Sometimes those
who protest the loudest are the nearest to the kingdom. Sometimes
the heart prepares the way for the mind to follow. In that way,
Trumpkin is a bit like Lewis himself, who embraced the beauty
and order of God's world and the stories in it long before he finally
embraced "the True Myth" of the gospel. Such preparation is sometimes essential in shaping our minds and making our hearts ready
to embrace the truth.

As Lewis's hero George MacDonald once put it (and as the
children's journey to Aslan behind Lucy's leadership demonstrates),
"Obedience is the great opener of eyes." Or in the words of Jesus, "If
anyone's will is to do God's will, he will know whether the teaching
is from God" (John 7:17). Just ask Trumpkin.

5

The Lost Art of Chivalry

Recovering the Virtues of Ferocity and Meekness

Lewis loved chivalry, that special contribution of the Christian Middle Ages to the modern world. In particular, he regarded chivalry as a necessity for lasting happiness and dignity in society. Indeed, at one point he (perhaps hyperbolically) called it "the one hope of the world."

Lewis recognized the crucial importance of the double demand that the chivalric ideal makes on human nature.

> The knight is a man of blood and iron, a man familiar with the sight of smashed faces and the ragged stumps of lopped-off limbs; he is also a demure, almost a maidenlike, guest in hall, a gentle, modest, unobtrusive man. He is not a compromise or happy mean between ferocity and meekness; he is fierce to the *n*th and meek to the *n*th.[20]

This combination of ferocity and meekness, restricted to the appropriate occasions and situations, is necessary because humanity is otherwise prone to fall into two main groups: bloodthirsty wolves and cowardly lambs. Lewis reads the history of the world as essentially a cyclical progression in which cruel barbarians rape, pillage, and destroy a civilization, only to settle in to become soft and decadent, unable to resist the onslaught of the next barbarian hordes. Chivalry, with its dual demand on men, sought to break this cycle by creating lion-like lambs and lamb-like lions.

> The medieval ideal brought together two things which have no natural tendency to gravitate towards one another. It brought them together for that very reason. It taught humility and forbearance to the great warrior because everyone knew by experience how much he usually needed that lesson. It demanded valour of the urbane and modest man because everyone knew that he was as likely as not to be a milksop.[21]

This ideal, covering as it does a whole host of human existence and social situations—from the savage clash of swords in battle to the minutiae of manners when meeting a woman for the first time—is not something that just happens. It is "art not nature," which means it must be taught, encouraged, and cultivated. It is just this sort of instruction in chivalry and knighthood that Lewis sets out to do in *Prince Caspian*, especially through the character of the High King Peter.

Chivalry on the Battlefield

While the martial elements of knighthood are not as prominent in *Prince Caspian*, Peter does acquit himself well in his battle with Miraz. To begin with, Peter demonstrates great courage and strategic wisdom in his willingness to fight the older and battle-hardened Miraz in single combat. Simply by challenging Miraz to single combat, he hopes to create some time so that he can "inspect the army and strengthen the position." Even if Miraz rejected the challenge, the delay might afford Aslan the opportunity to do something (Ch. 13).

His written challenge to Miraz is a model of courtly language ("For to prevent the effusion of blood. . . ."), deliberate provocation ("Wherefore we most heartily provoke, challenge, and defy your Lordship to the said combat and monomachy"), and subtle insults (he says that Miraz is only "styling himself King of Narnia").

His actual combat in battle is likewise a picture of knightly shrewdness and bravery. Despite Miraz's height and weight advantage, Peter draws first blood. He uses his own youth and stamina to his advantage by keeping out of range of Miraz in hopes of wearing him down in the hot sun, resisting the taunts of "Coward!" by the Telmarines as he "dances" with the older warrior. When he's knocked down by Miraz and all seems lost, he uses Miraz's own arm as a ladder in order to regain his feet. Even when injured, he never loses his composure or shows fear, but instead tells Edmund to give everyone his love in the event of his death. Finally, when Miraz trips on some grass, Peter refrains from pressing the advantage, but instead steps back to allow Miraz to rise. Edmund attributes such honorable conduct in battle to the fact that Peter is both "a Knight *and* a High King," remarking that it is just the sort of conduct that Aslan would like (Ch. 14).

Chivalry on the Home Front

Far more important (and in many cases, more directly applicable) than Peter's embodiment of the war-like virtues in *Prince Caspian* is his demonstration of the chivalric qualities outside of battle. First, Peter shows an intentional concern for the dignity of others. When the four children consider whether to swim across the channel to the mainland, Peter includes himself in the ones who would have trouble swimming. "'It would be all right for Su,' said Peter (Susan had won prizes for swimming at school). 'But I don't know about the rest of us.' By 'the rest of us' he really meant Edmund who couldn't yet do two lengths at the school baths, and Lucy, who could hardly swim at all" (Ch. 3). In doing so, he avoids placing unnecessary blame on his two younger siblings.

Second, Peter tactfully controls his own temper and wisely manages potential conflict among the group. When Edmund takes offense at Trumpkin's dismissal of the siblings, it's Peter that says, "There's no good losing our tempers." Later, when Trumpkin condescendingly doubts that Lucy has seen Aslan, Peter prevents her from attacking the Dwarf by reminding her that Trumpkin doesn't understand Aslan and then gently rebukes the Dwarf for speaking nonsense about the great Lion. Most importantly, when the children and the Dwarf seem lost in their search for the Rush River, and Peter is frustrated with his own leadership, he still manages to keep his temper, even if it is "with some difficulty" (Ch. 9). The key is that Peter is a skillful leader who knows how both to control his own temper and to diffuse potentially explosive situations.

Third, Peter understands and embraces his role in the story. Though he is the High King over all kings of Narnia, he does not lord it over the others nor compete with Caspian. In fact, the first words out of his mouth when he meets the young Prince are, "I haven't come to take your place, you know, but to put you into it" (Ch. 12). What's more, when Aslan informs him and Susan that they will not be returning to Narnia, Peter is puzzled but not resistant. He embraces the fact that it's time to go home and grow up and live like a Narnian in England (Ch. 15).

Finally, Peter shows an appropriate sense of decorum, generosity, and magnanimity. He acknowledges the badger's faithfulness by kissing him on the head when he first meets him. He honors the Bear's ancient right to serve as a Marshal of the List, even if the Bear has the potential to bring shame on the army by sucking his paws. He seeks to cheer up the Giant Wimbleweather after his blunders in battle by sending him as an escort with his challenge to Miraz. He skillfully handles Reepicheep's request to serve as a Marshal, denying the Mouse's desire while maintaining his dignity.

He even commands that Nikabrik be buried according to Dwarfish custom, despite his evil and treachery (Ch. 13).

All of these examples may seem small and insignificant in the grand scheme of things. After all, isn't the important thing that he fight bravely and win the battle? But their smallness is precisely the point. For manners, whether in the court or at the dinner table, are simply love in the little things, love in the trifles.

The Perfect Knight

It is this deliberate concern with courtesy, honor, and the dignity of others that is so necessary for us if we are to live like true Narnians in our homes, in our churches, and in the world. Our Lord requires that husbands show honor to their wives as the weaker vessel (1 Pet. 3:7), and that wives respect and honor their husbands as their head (Eph. 5:33). Children likewise must honor their parents (Ex. 20:12), and parents must imitate God in remembering the frame of their children (Psa. 103:14) and not provoking or discouraging them (Col. 3:21). All Christians are called to sacrificially serve one another rather than lording our authority or rights over each other like the unbelievers do (Matt. 20:25–28). Elders in particular are singled out as those who must not be domineering over those in their charge, but instead be, like the High King Peter, an example to the flock (1 Pet. 5:3).

In all of this, our ultimate model is the Lord Jesus himself, the one who protects the accused from the stones of hypocrites, who washes the filthy feet of Galilean fishermen, and who drives the wicked from his Father's house with zeal. Having served others and given his life as a ransom for many, he promises to return in wrath and repay with affliction those who have assaulted his people. For he is the true embodiment of chivalry, the perfect Knight above all knights. It is he that truly combines in himself the paradox of ferocity and meekness. He is the Conquering Lion of Judah and the Humble Lamb that was Slain.

6

The Folly of Nothing-Buttery

There's Always More Than Meets the Eye

We live in an age of scientific reductionism, a time when *material* causes are assumed to be the *only* causes. We presume (and it is a presumption) that if we have discovered the mechanism of a thing, that we now understand the complete nature of the thing. Indeed, we operate on the assumption that, if we could exhaustively understand the material forces and causes at work in, say, the body of a dog, that we thereby exhaustively understand the dog itself.

I call this view scientific reductionism because it reduces things to their material components and properties, leaving no room for anything beyond the physical. The world and all it contains is simply chemicals in motion, atoms banging about, molecules flying every which way (some of them singing and fighting and praying and eating, as flying molecules are wont to do).

The proper term for this type of reductionism is "nothing-buttery" since everything that we can see and know is "nothing but" a mixture of matter in motion. Humans are "nothing but" sacks of protoplasm (children being smaller and cuter sacks, more like "baggies of protoplasm"). Love is "nothing but" a chemical reaction in someone's brain. Far from being "man's best friend," a dog is "nothing but" the current product of a random evolutionary process that is leading us "nobody knows where." And a star is "nothing but" a huge ball of flaming gas.

Explaining without Explaining Away

Which, of course, brings us to *The Voyage of the Dawn Treader*. For Lewis was at war with "nothing-buttery" not only because it is false, but because it is ugly, degrading, and harmful to human flourishing. In *The Abolition of Man*, Lewis laments the way in which modern science, like the late medieval pursuit of magic, is an attempt to conquer nature, "to subdue reality to the wishes of men" through technique and technology. In seeking to extend "Man's power to all things possible," Man ceases to be Man, being conquered *by* Nature in the very act of conquering Nature, since Nature—now restricted to those phenomena and features that are scientifically testable and capable of manipulation—eventually swallows up Man himself, reducing him to his physical and material components. Man does gain mastery over Nature, but in the process he forfeits his soul.[22]

Lewis proposes a different sort of approach to the Natural World, what he calls "regenerate science."

> The regenerate science which I have in mind would not do even to minerals and vegetables what modern science threatens to do to man himself. When it explained it would not explain away. When it spoke of the parts it would remember the whole. While studying the *It* it would not lose what Martin Buber calls the *Thou*-situation. The analogy between the *Tao* of Man and the instincts of an animal species would mean for it new light cast on the unknown thing, Instinct, by the only known reality of conscience and not a reduction of conscience to the category of Instinct. Its followers would not be free with the words *only* and *merely*. In a word, it would conquer Nature without being at the

same time conquered by her and buy knowledge at a lower cost than that of life.[23]

"When it explained it would not explain away." "Its followers would not be free with the words *only* and *merely*." It is this lesson that Eustace learns in his conversation with Ramandu.

"I saw them long ago," said the Old Man, "but it was from a great height. I cannot tell you such things as sailors need to know."

"Do you mean you were flying in the air?" Eustace blurted out.

"I was a long way above the air, my son," replied the Old Man. "I am Ramandu. But I see that you stare at one another and have not heard this name. And no wonder, for the days when I was a star had ceased long before any of you knew this world, and all the constellations have changed."

"Golly," said Edmund under his breath. "He's a retired star."

"Aren't you a star any longer?" asked Lucy.

"I am a star at rest, my daughter," answered Ramandu. "When I set for the last time, decrepit and old beyond all that you can reckon, I was carried to this island. I am not so old now as I was then. Every morning a bird brings me a fire-berry from the valleys in the Sun, and each fire-berry takes away a little of my age. And when I have become as young as the child that was born yesterday, then I shall take my rising again (for we are at earth's eastern rim) and once more tread the great dance."

"In our world," said Eustace, "a star is a huge ball of flaming gas."

"Even in your world, my son, that is not what a star is but only what it is made of.

In Narnia, a star is *more* than a ball of flaming gas. Stars can appear as old men or a beautiful princess. They can retire for a season before rejoining the heavenly procession. They can apparently commit faults and be punished and restored. And according to Ramandu (and Lewis), something like this is true in our world as well. Yes, stars are truly made of flaming gas, burning brilliantly in the distant sky. But even the stars of our world transcend their physical properties.

Are Stars Really More Than Balls of Gas?

For me, Ramandu's line is enigmatic and suggestive, awakening questions of wonder in my heart and mind. It causes me to ask, "What, then, is a star, if it is more than flaming gas?" And, perhaps unsurprisingly, the reader of Scripture will find that our stars may be more like Narnian stars than we'd ever thought possible. Here are a few suggestive hints.

In the book of Judges, Deborah and Barak sing a war hymn, celebrating God's victory over the Canaanite king Sisera. One line in the song reads, "From heaven the stars fought, from their courses they fought against Sisera" (Judg. 5:19). A metaphor? Perhaps. But even metaphors shouldn't be tagged with words like "mere" or "only," as if they were somehow "lesser" than non-metaphorical speech. Biblical metaphors aren't merely creative ways to communicate; they are deeply and fundamentally true, divinely designed analogies that enable us to more fully understand God and his world. So at the very least, let us not denigrate and dismiss metaphors as beneath us in our scientific and "enlightened" age. Describing things by multiplying metaphors and analogies is often a far superior way of coming to truly understand something, than attempting to strip away all of its features through reductionistic definitions. And, in Sisera's case, we should also stay open to the possibility that Deborah's line is as much history as it is poetry.

Even more provocative are passages like Job 38:7, in which "the morning stars sang together and all the sons of God shouted for joy" over God's act of creation (Lewis depicts a Narnian version of this scene in *The Magician's Nephew*). Earlier in the book of Job, the sons of God including Satan present themselves before God in heaven (2:6). Thus it seems likely that the morning stars and sons of God in Job 38 are angelic beings. This identification of stars and angels fits well with Micaiah's heavenly vision in 1 Kings 22:19, where the prophet sees the Lord on his throne with "all the host of heaven standing beside him on his right hand and his left." In the Old Testament, the "host of heaven" is a common designation for stars and planets (Deut. 4:19; 17:3; Jer. 8:2; 33:22; Neh. 9:6), but also includes false gods worshiped by the nations (Isa. 24:21; 2 Kings 16:16; 21:3). In the book of Revelation, the Dragon sweeps one third of the stars from the sky and casts them to earth (Rev. 12:4). Thus, again the Bible links the stars with angelic beings, in this case with fallen angels who follow the devil in his rebellion.

Finally, some biblical scholars argue that the star of Bethlehem is best understood as an angelic being who comes to guide the magi to the house where Jesus was (note that the star "came to rest over the place where the child was," Matt. 2:9, a remarkable feat if it is simply a ball of flaming gas billions of light years away). Similarly, when the angel announces the birth of Jesus to the shepherds in Luke 2:9–12, he is immediately joined by "a multitude of the heavenly host" who sing praise to God before going "away from them into heaven" (2:13–15). Perhaps, like Ramandu, angelic stars are able to appear on earth in a human form and then return back to their blazing spheres of hydrogen and helium.

Opening Us to Wonderful Mysteries

The point of this brief and suggestive Bible study is to echo and affirm the wisdom of Ramandu and to instill in us the truth that "nothing-buttery" is as unbiblical as it is un-Narnian. By all means, let us explore the physical and material world, wisely and faithfully using the tools of science to discover how the world works. But let us never fall prey to the seductive reductionism that explains away the wonders of God's world. Let us resist with every fiber of our being the banality of restricting reality to those things that we can weigh and measure with our fancy instruments.

Let us instead read our fairy stories and learn from them as Chesterton did. "These tales say that apples were golden only to refresh the forgotten moment when we found that they were green. They make rivers run with wine only to make us remember, for one wild moment, that they run with water."[24]

Or again,

> The only words that ever satisfied me as describing Nature are the terms used in the fairy books, "charm," "spell," "enchantment." They express the arbitrariness of the fact and its mystery. A tree grows fruit because it is a *magic* tree. Water runs downhill because it is bewitched.[25]

For this also is what it means to live like a Narnian. It means to greet the world the way that you'd great a retired star, to resolve to see the world the way that Lewis scholar Clyde Kilby did:

Resolved:

1. At least once every day I shall look steadily up at the sky and remember that I, a consciousness with a conscience, am on a planet traveling in space with wonderfully mysterious things above and about me.

6. I shall open my eyes and ears. Once every day I shall simply stare at a tree, a flower, a cloud, or a person. I shall not then be concerned at all to ask what they are but simply be glad that they are. I shall joyfully allow them the mystery of what Lewis calls their "divine, magical, terrifying and ecstatic" existence.

7. I shall sometimes look back at the freshness of vision I had in childhood and try, at least for a little while, to be, in the words of Lewis Carroll, the "child of the pure unclouded brow, and dreaming eyes of wonder."[26]

7

⌒

After Darkness, Light

Seeing Everything by the Light of the Lion

Lewis was a man familiar with Darkness. More importantly (and tragically), his familiarity with Darkness began when he was a child. His mother died when he was nine, an event which would mark him for the rest of his life. During his childhood he suffered from night-terrors, which he called "a private hell," and thus was sensitive to the danger of inflaming terror in children. He survived the trenches of France during World War I (though he was injured in battle). His close friend Paddy Moore was not so fortunate. Later in life, Lewis lost his beloved wife Joy to cancer (he records his wrestling with the darkness of her loss in *A Grief Observed*). And of course, beyond the darkness of pain and loss was the darkness of indwelling sin, that 'red lizard' that tempts, pleads, and eventually destroys us.[27]

But more than darkness, Lewis had come to know (or rather come to be known) by the Light. His blind eyes had been opened so that he was able to see the light of the knowledge of the glory of God in the face of Christ. He had come to embrace the truth that "the light shines in the darkness, and the darkness has not over-come it" (John 1:5). Light and Sight. This is what *The Voyage of the Dawn Treader* is all about.

Scattering the Darkness with Aslan's Light

For starters, the entire story is a journey eastward toward the ever-enlarging sun. As they near the Utter East, the characters are able to endure the brightness of the sun only because they drink the sweet water of the world's Last Sea. "Drinkable light" is what they call it, and it not only gives them eagle eyes with which to view the sun shining in its full strength, it actually causes them to shine them-selves ("their own faces and bodies became brighter and brighter," Ch. 15).

But the importance of Light in the story goes beyond the direc-tion of the boat and the sun's rays. The heart of the story is the characters' growing ability to see light in Aslan's Light, to have their darkness scattered by the brightness of the great Lion, to not only see Aslan, but by him to see everything else.

The most obvious example of Aslan's power to enlighten the darkness is the rescue of Lord Rhoop from Dark Island. The island where dreams come true is no paradise; it is an endless nightmare. When the crew realized the significance of Lord Rhoop's insistence that dreams—not daydreams, but real dreams—come true on the island,

> There was about half a minute's silence and then, with a great clatter of armor, the whole crew were tumbling down the main hatch as quick as they could and flinging themselves on the oars to row as they had never rowed before; and Drinian was swinging round the tiller, and the boat-swain was giving out the quickest stroke that had ever been heard at sea.
>
> For it had taken everyone just that half-minute to remember certain dreams they had had—dreams that make you afraid of going to sleep

again—and to realize what it would mean to land on a country where dreams come true. (Ch. 12)

One detects Lewis's own experience with night-terrors behind the fear of the crew: the fear of close friends turning into something horrible, of things crawling up the side of the ship, of the noise of gongs (and even scissors). The horror of the darkness and the terrible prospect of no escape leads Rhoop to scream and Lucy to whisper a desperate prayer: "Aslan, Aslan, if ever you loved us at all, send us help now."

Immediately a beam of light appears, with something like a cross in it (it turns out to be an albatross). The bird circles and sings in a strong sweet voice, whispering, "Courage, dear heart," to Lucy as it passes. With the albatross as a guide, the ship bursts into the sunlight, to the great relief of the crew who realized "that there was nothing to be afraid of and never had been." They all share a laugh at how foolish they'd all been, and then turn around to discover that "the Dark Island and the darkness had vanished forever" (Ch. 12).

The Alternative Version of the Rescue from Dark Island

This at least is how the original British edition and most modern editions (which are based on it) describe their escape. However, Lewis revised this section when the book was first released in America. The alternative section reads like this (additional text in **bold**):

> In a few moments the darkness turned into a grayness ahead, and then, almost before they dared to begin hoping, they had shot out into the sunlight and were in the warm, blue world again. **And just as there are moments when simply to lie in bed and see the daylight pouring through your window and to hear the cheerful voice of an early post-man or milkman down below and to realize that** *it was only a dream: it wasn't real,* **is so heavenly that it was very nearly worth having the**

nightmare in order to have the joy of waking; so they all felt when they came out of the dark. The brightness of the ship herself astonished them: they had half expected to find that the darkness would cling to the white and the green and the gold in the form of some grime or scum.

Lucy lost no time in coming down to the deck, where she found the others all gathered round the newcomer. For a long time he was too happy to speak, and could only gaze at the sea and the sun and feel the bulwarks and the ropes, as if to make sure he was really awake, while tears rolled down his cheeks.

"Thank you," he said at last. "You have saved me from ... but I won't talk of that. And now let me know who you are. I am a Telmarine of Narnia, and when I was worth anything men called me the Lord Rhoop."

"And I," said Caspian, "am Caspian, King of Narnia, and I sail to find you and your companions who were my father's friends."

Lord Rhoop fell on his knees and kissed the King's hand. "Sire," he said, "you are the man in all the world I most wished to see. Grant me a boon."

"What is it?" asked Caspian.

"Never to ask me, nor to let any other ask me, what I have seen during my years on the Dark Island."

"An easy boon, my Lord," answered Caspian, and added with a shudder. "*Ask* you: I should think not. I would give all my treasure *not* to hear it."

"Sire," said Drinian, "this wind is fair for the southeast. Shall I have our poor fellows up and set sail? And after that, every man who can be spared, to his hammock."

"Yes," said Caspian, "and let there be grog all round. Heigh-ho, I feel I could sleep the clock round myself."

So all afternoon with great joy they sailed southeast with a fair wind and the hump of darkness grew smaller and smaller astern.[28]

Gone is the easy, almost flippant dismissal of the Dark Island and its nightmares. The terrors of the night are not to be dismissed so lightly. However, the joy of waking, the joy of morning, is almost enough to make the nightmare worth it. Moreover, the effects of such terrors can linger during the day, even as they grow smaller and smaller the farther we move from them. In both cases, Aslan's Light is the cause of our deliverance. Because of him, we need not fear the terrors of the night, nor the arrows that fly by day, nor the pestilence that stalks in darkness, nor the destruction that wastes at noonday.

The Sin-Killing Power of the Lion's Light

But the Light of Aslan delivers from more than simply nightmares and dark islands. Aslan, with moonlight shining around him on a moonless night, de-dragons an insufferable young man (Ch. 7). The sight of the huge lion "shining as if he were in bright sunlight though the sun had in fact gone in," delivers Edmund and Caspian from greed and deadly rivalry on Deathwater Island (Ch. 8). Seeing Aslan's bright but growling face in the Magician's book kills Lucy's vanity and covetous desire for physical beauty (Ch. 10). And the golden face of the Lion rebukes and humbles Caspian's stubbornness and Miraz-like pride when he seeks to abandon his post as King for the sake of private adventures (Ch. 16).

In all of these instances, the sight of the Bright and Shining Lion leads to repentance and restoration, scattering the darkness of sin and disobedience. In Aslan is Light, and his light is the light of men, shining in the darkness, unable to be overcome. Like Jesus, he is the Light of the World, and in another beautiful twist from the writings of the Apostle John, he is the Lamb of God, who takes away the sins of the world, the Lion of Judah who scatters light from his mane, the one who answers Edmund's question about whether he is in our world too with the simple phrase:

"I am."

8

Parents, Educrats, and Bureaucrats

Lewis's Subtle Assault on Progressivism

Some aspects of Narnian discipleship are obvious, like the value of courage and sacrifice. Others are more subtle. One of Lewis's more subtle aims appears to be to train us (and particularly children) to be suspicious of modern myths, particularly the peculiar modern Myth of Progress. Central to this Myth is Developmentalism, the application of Evolution to all spheres of life—physical, social, political, and religious—so that everything is not merely changing, but perpetually improving. The Myth of Progress dismisses "traditional morality," "practical reason," and "natural law" (what Lewis sometimes refers to as the *Tao*) because it is old and outdated. In its place Progress erects science (or more accurately, scientism), statism, and the humanitarian theory of punishment.

The Tyranny of the Humanitarian Theory of Punishment

The humanitarian theory of punishment does away with traditional notions of "desert" and "retributive justice" in favor of punishment as deterrent and cure. Crime is viewed in pathological terms, as a disease in need of mending, rather than as an evil act in need of just punishment. This view of punishment has the appearance of mercy, but in reality is wholly false.

> The Humanitarian theory wants simply to abolish Justice and substitute Mercy for it. This means that you start being 'kind' to people before you have considered their rights, and then force upon them supposed kindnesses which no one but you will recognize as kindnesses and which the recipient will feel as abominable cruelties. You have overshot the mark. Mercy, detached from Justice, grows unmerciful.[29]

The dangers of this theory are manifold. It removes considerations of punishment and sentencing from ordinary juries and society as a whole and places them in the hands of technical experts and doctors, those who are qualified to determine how to "heal" the "disease" of crime. By removing justice from the equation, it creates the possibility (and indeed likelihood) that innocent people will be falsely "convicted" for exemplary purposes, so that others may be deterred by their punishment. It deprives the criminal of the rights of a human being, since he can now be "treated" for his neurosis for as long as it takes to cure him.

The tyranny of the Humanitarian theory does not depend on the evil intentions of its practitioners. Indeed, Lewis argues that the Humanitarian theory is what enables otherwise good men to do unspeakably evil things.

> My contention is that good men (not bad men) consistently acting upon that position would act as cruelly and unjustly as the greatest tyrants. They might in some respects act even worse. Of all tyrannies a

tyranny sincerely exercised for the good of its victims may be the most oppressive. It may be better to live under robber barons than under omnipotent moral busybodies. The robber baron's cruelty may sometimes sleep, his cupidity may at some point be satiated; but those who torment us for our own good will torment us without end for they do so with the approval of their own conscience. They may be more likely to go to Heaven yet at the same time likelier to make a Hell of earth.[30]

Lewis regarded it as "essential to oppose the Humanitarian theory of punishment, root and branch, wherever we encounter it." He thought that such theories were bound together with notions of government in which the State "exists not to protect our rights but to do us good or make us good." The State's role in providing such "goods and services" necessitated an increasingly large bureaucratic government, one that inevitably enslaves its citizens.

Two wars necessitated vast curtailments of liberty and we have grown, though grumblingly, accustomed to our chains. The increasing complexity and precariousness of our economic life have forced Government to take over many spheres of activity once left to choice or chance....There is nothing left of which we can say to [our new leaders], 'Mind your own business.' Our whole lives are their business.[31]

It is these Progressive, Humanitarian, and Statist notions that lie beneath the surface of some of Lewis's descriptions and characterizations in *The Voyage of the Dawn Treader* and *The Silver Chair*. Lewis did not expect children to be able to understand the dangers of progressivism, humanitarianism, or statism, or to even understand what these various modern idolatries were. But he did hope to inculcate in them a healthy suspicion of their proponents by including snapshots of them in his books.

Three Spheres: Family, School, and State

The first snapshot is the Scrubb family: Harold, Alberta, and (before he was transformed by breathing Narnian air) Eustace. Lewis describes them as "very up-to-date and advanced people" (that is, progressive), so much so that their son calls them by their first names rather than "Mother or Father." They were "vegetarians, non-smokers and teetotalers," and they were austere when it came to furniture and clothing (one thinks of a sanitized version of the White Witch). From his parents, Eustace seems to have imbibed pacifism (he refuses to have a duel with Reepicheep), egalitarianism (he's a "Republican" who has some anti-monarchical sentiment), and feminism (when Lucy is given the King's quarters because she is a girl, Eustace quotes his mother to the effect that "all that sort of thing is really lowering girls," *The Voyage of the Dawn Treader*, Chs. 1–2).

The second snapshot is the school that the Scrubbs send Eustace to. It's called "Experiment House," presumably because it adopts modern experimental methods of education, "curious methods" that don't teach French or Math or Latin very well and leave Eustace severely impoverished when it comes to knowledge of dragons. The school rejects corporal punishment, discourages Bible reading, and was "Co-educational"—again, all elements that testify to the progressive ideology that lies beneath the surface. The distinguishing mark as far as the children are concerned is that the people who ran the school "had the idea that boys and girls should be allowed to do what they liked" (*The Silver Chair*, Ch. 1) In other words, rather than setting boundaries and training children in the ways of traditional morality and classical education, the teachers and administration allowed the children to follow their natural inclinations, which essentially meant that the biggest children bullied the rest. Lewis no doubt intends this as a microcosm and foretaste of the future of society if the Progressive Innovators that he identifies in *The Abolition of Man* are allowed to run the show.

The Headmistress of Experiment House views the bullies as "interesting psychological cases," thus betraying her allegiance to the Humanitarian theory of crime and punishment. Like the Elderly Lady Judge in one of Lewis's essays, she most likely treats harsh and harmful bullying as an example of "stupid pranks" and ends up using the Rules to protect the bullies rather than their victims, so that the bullies were in fact her favorites.[32] Her eventual failure as a Head results in her promotion to Inspector and then to Parliament "where she lived happily ever after" (Ch. 16).

The move from school to government highlights Lewis's third snapshot of Progressivism. Governor Gumpas of the Lone Islands is a "chickenhearted man" who is always "muddling and messing about with accounts and forms and rules and regulations." He is the consummate bureaucrat, objecting to Caspian's arrival with talk of appointments, applications, and commissions of inquiry. He justifies the thriving slave trade in his territory as an unavoidable, economic necessity, "essential to the economic development of the islands" and duly supported by graphs and statistics. When Caspian unilaterally ends the trade and frees the slaves, Gumpas objects in the name of "progress" and "development" (Ch. 4).

Gumpas is the Narnian demonstration of Lewis's words in the Preface to *Screwtape Letters*, in which he explains why he depicts the devils as paper-pushing administrators:

> I like bats much better than bureaucrats. I live in the Managerial Age, in a world of 'Admin.' The greatest evil is not now done in those sordid 'dens of crime' that Dickens loved to paint. It is not done even in concentration camps and labour camps. In those we see its final result. But it is conceived and ordered (moved, seconded, carried, and minuted) in clean, carpeted, warmed, and well-lighted offices, by quiet men with white collars and cut fingernails and smooth-shaven cheeks who do not need to raise their voice. Hence, naturally enough, my symbol for Hell is something like the bureaucracy of a police state or the offices of a thoroughly nasty business concern.[33]

Lewis greatly feared that the danger of hunger, the dread of war, and the increasing complexity of the global economy would lead citizens to make a "terrible bargain," to trade liberty for the promise of security and stability. Ancient man sold himself as a slave in order to eat, embraced the witch-doctor in order to save himself from the sorcerer, or relied on the warlord to stave off the barbarians. Now the modern, technocratic state offers us the hope of economic stability and permanent employment, if we will only become willing slaves of the Welfare State.

The Beauty of the Freeborn Mind

By portraying, however obliquely, the ugliness of the modern -isms, Lewis hoped to create in young people an immunity to their seductive power. More than that, the Narnian Chronicles are designed to instill a different vision of human life and society—a fuller, richer, and happier one built on what Lewis called "the freeborn mind."

> To live his life in his own way, to call his house his castle, to enjoy the fruits of his own labour, to educate his children as his conscience directs, to save for their prosperity after his death—these are the wishes deeply ingrained in white and civilized man. Their realization is almost as necessary to our virtues as to our happiness. From their total frustration disastrous results both moral and psychological might follow.[34]

This passage finds an echo in the description of the four Great Kings and Queens in *The Lion, the Witch, and the Wardrobe*. The reign of Peter, Susan, Edmund, and Lucy was a long and happy one, and one of the key features that Lewis highlights is that they "made good laws and kept the peace ... and generally stopped busybodies and interferers and encouraged ordinary people who wanted to live and let live" (*The Lion, the Witch, and the Wardrobe*, Ch. 17).

In the Scrubbs, Experiment House, and Gumpas we see the anti-Narnia, the distorted alternative that spurs us on to more fully pursue a robustly Christian vision of the family, of education, and of society. The question for us is whether children who read Narnia would recognize us in the Scrubbs or in the Pevensies, in Experiment House or in Dr. Cornelius, in Gumpas or in Lord Bern. For living like a Narnian is no individualistic affair; our families, our schools, our churches and communities must also come to reflect the nobility, liberty, order, and beauty of Aslan and his people.

9

Breaking Enchantments with Burnt Marshwiggle

Defending the Faith against Modern Fables

One of the more impressive feats of the Narnian books is Lewis's ability to seamlessly incorporate arguments from his apologetic works throughout the stories. An obvious example is Professor Kirke's line of reasoning about Lucy in his conversation with Peter and Susan in *The Lion, the Witch, and the Wardrobe*. The older children don't believe that Lucy has been in Narnia, and Edmund, who had joined her there, says that they were just playing make-believe. Lucy's miserable reaction leads the older children to conclude that she might be losing her mind, so they discuss the matter with the Professor. Upon hearing that Lucy is generally truthful and observing that she is clearly not insane, the Professor startles the children with some surprising words.

"Logic!" said the Professor half to himself. "Why don't they teach logic at these schools? There are only three possibilities. Either your sister is telling lies, or she is mad, or she is telling the truth. You know she doesn't tell lies and it is obvious that she is not mad. For the moment then and unless any further evidence turns up, we must assume that she is telling the truth." (*The Lion, the Witch, and the Wardrobe*, Ch. 5)

For readers of Lewis's apologetic works, the structure of the Professor's argument is very familiar. It's identical to Lewis's famous "Liar, Lunatic, or Lord" argument from *Mere Christianity*.

I am trying here to prevent anyone saying the really foolish thing that people often say about Him: 'I'm ready to accept Jesus as a great moral teacher, but I don't accept His claim to be God.' That is the one thing we must not say. A man who was merely a man and said the sort of things Jesus said would not be a great moral teacher. He would either be a lunatic—on a level with the man who says he is a poached egg—or else he would be the Devil of Hell. You must make your choice. Either this man was, and is, the Son of God: or else a madman or something worse. You can shut Him up for a fool, you can spit at Him and kill Him as a demon; or you can fall at His feet and call Him Lord and God. But let us not come with any patronising nonsense about His being a great human teacher. He has not left that open to us. He did not intend to.[35]

In mimicking the structure of this argument in *The Lion, the Witch, and the Wardrobe*, Lewis's aim seems to be to train the minds of his young readers to think in the proper categories for evaluating the claims of Christ. This is a kind of indirect apologetics, a softening of the soil before the planting of the seeds. Children who grow up with these types of categories and arguments in their mind will be well-prepared to receive (and defend) the biblical claims about the identity of Jesus.

Lewis does this sort of thing elsewhere in the Chronicles (for example, the horse Bree presents a de-historicized, spiritualized view of Aslan in *The Horse and His Boy*, similar to arguments that might be made about the full humanity and historicity of Christ). But the most extensive and impressive example of such apologetic category creation is found in *The Silver Chair.*

The Green Lady's Seductive Story

Jill, Eustace, and Puddleglum have found their way into Underland, where they meet the Black Knight, a friendly but mysterious character who is subservient to the Lady of the Green Kirtle. The Knight is revealed to be the lost Prince Rilian, who has been enchanted and bound by the Emerald Lady, who is really a witch. The Prince is freed from his enchantment by Puddleglum and the children, just as the Emerald Witch returns. When Rilian expresses their intention to leave Underland and return to Overland, the Witch throws some green powder in the fire, which produces a "sweet and drowsy smell," and begins to strum on an instrument. The combination of the incense and the strumming "made it hard to think" and the longer it went on, the less you noticed it and "the less you noticed it, the more it got into your brain and blood" (*The Silver Chair*, Ch. 12).

Once the smell and strumming have begun to work, the Witch begins questioning the group, sweetly and gently denying the existence of Narnia and all of Overland. When Eustace reminds her that they initially met her in Overland, the Witch dismisses him with a lovely laugh, saying, "I have no memory of that meeting. But we often meet our friends in strange places when we dream. And unless all dreamed alike, you must not ask them to remember it." She likewise dismisses Rilian's claim to be a Narnian prince and Jill's words about coming from Another World as mere dreams and pretty games.

As Rilian and the children succumb to the Witch's gentle enchantment, Puddleglum fights hard and boldly asserts the reality of Narnia and Overworld, saying, "I've seen the sky full of stars. I've seen the sun coming up out of the sea of a morning and sinking behind the mountains at night. And I've seen him up in the midday sky when I couldn't look at him for brightness" (Ch. 12). This rouses the others who likewise affirm their knowledge of the sun.

The Lady gently asks them what they mean by "sun," and Rilian responds by pointing to a lamp and saying, "Now that thing which we call the sun is like the lamp, only far greater and brighter. It giveth light to the whole Overworld and hangeth in the sky." The Witch cleverly responds by showing that the Prince's analogy with the lamp simply proves that "Your sun is a dream; and there is nothing in that dream that was not copied from the lamp. The lamp is the real thing; the sun is but a tale, a children's story." The Witch's words, working with the enchanted smell and the magic strumming, convince them that the sun is simply a figment of their imaginations.

Then Jill, struggling to fight against the enchantment, says, "There's Aslan." When the Witch learns that he is a lion, she asks what a lion is. Eustace responds that a lion is "like a huge cat—with a mane. At least, it's not like a horse's mane, you know, it's more like a judge's wig. And it's yellow. And terrifically strong."

Again, the Witch turns the table on the Narnians:

> "I see," she said, "that we should do no better with your lion, as you call it, than we did with your sun. You have seen lamps, and so you imagined a bigger and better lamp and called it the sun. You've seen cats, and now you want a bigger and better cat, and it's to be called a lion. Well, 'tis a pretty make-believe, though, to say truth, it would suit you all better if you were younger. And look how you can put nothing into your make-believe without copying it from the real world, this world of mine, which is the only world." (*The Silver Chair*, Ch. 12)

She then rebukes the Prince and the children for playing such childish games and urges them to have a deep sleep and "begin a wiser life tomorrow."

The Fables of Feuerbach and Freud

Now before describing how Lewis resolves this situation in the book, it's important to note what lies behind this conversation. The unseen, but very real opponents that Lewis is engaging with are 19th and 20th century thinkers who sought to undermine Christianity through what's called the psychogenetic method. This method of argument is associated with thinkers like Ludwig Feuerbach and Sigmund Freud, and still survives in various forms today.[36]

These thinkers argued that human beings have created God in our own image, as a projection of our own yearnings, needs, and desires. Feuerbach famously argued that if God were a being of the birds, he would have been a winged creature. In this sense, the Christian God is simply another man-made idol and should be toppled so that man can learn to believe in himself. Their basic goal was to replace God with Man, urging people to give up childish ways and grow up into adulthood.

Since God is merely a projection of human ideals, psychogenetic thinkers sought to identify the human needs met by God, explain the origin of belief in God in terms of those needs, and thereby undermine the belief's validity and cause its power to dissipate. If belief in God can be explained in terms of primitive psychological and social needs (or today, in terms of biological or genetic causes), then it should be possible to find some other way to meet the need and then dispense with God altogether.

The following account of the origins of belief in God provides a perfect example of the psychogenetic method in action. Freud argues that, when we are children, we are dependent upon our parents, and come to see them (especially our fathers) as strong protectors who provide us with food, shelter, physical safety, and emotional security. As we grow up, we discover that our fathers are not as all-powerful as we thought, and that they too have failures and weaknesses. But in realizing the weaknesses of our fathers, we still have a psychological need for security and provision; we want to know that someone strong and loving is looking out for us. So, we project our fathers into the sky and create "God our Father," thus giving ourselves the illusion of control. Good things that happen to us are attributed to God's love and approval, bad things to his anger and judgment. Freud then suggests that we should put this childish belief in God behind us since a) we now know where it comes from, and b) through science and technology, we are capable of mastering Nature and standing on our own two feet.

Note the parallels between Feuerbach and Freud and the Green Lady. For Freud, God the Father is simply a copy and projection of earthly fatherhood, just as the sun is a fictional copy and projection of the lamp, and Aslan the Lion is simply a bigger and better cat. Likewise, Rilian and the children are rebuked for their childishness and urged to grow up, just as modern man should act like men and leave behind the crutch of a Heavenly Father (one also hears the folly of "nothing-buttery" in the Witch's confession that her world is the only world). Finally, the Witch's psychogenetic argument is depicted as a seductive enchantment, an alternative story that receives its power from bad magic. In his famous sermon, *The Weight of Glory*, after beautifully describing the echo of "our far-off country" that we all experience in and through the beauties and glories of this world, Lewis then says,

> Do you think I am trying to weave a spell? Perhaps I am; but remember your fairy tales. Spells are used for breaking enchantments as well as for inducing them. And you and I have need of the strongest spell that can be found to wake us from the evil enchantment of worldliness which has been laid upon us for nearly a hundred years.[37]

Modernism, with its alternative psychogenetic story of Religion and its myth of Progress and Creative Evolution, is simply an intoxicating enchantment that numbs us and lulls us to sleep. It is this sort of philosophy that Lewis is seeking to train us to defend against. To see how, we must return to Underland.

Puddleglum's Pain-Filled Rebuttal

With the enchantment almost complete and Rilian and the children falling deeper and deeper under the Witch's psychogenetic spell, all seems lost, until Puddleglum summons his strength, walks to the fragrant fire, and stamps his bare foot on it, filling the room with the unpleasant aroma of burnt Marsh-wiggle. This immediately begins to clear the heads of the others, awakens the anger of the Witch, and gives Puddleglum a moment of perfect clarity ("There is nothing like a good shock of pain for dissolving certain kinds of magic").

"One word, Ma'am," he said, coming back from the fire; limping, because of the pain. "One word. All you've been saying is quite right, I shouldn't wonder. I'm a chap who always liked to know the worst and then put the best face I can on it. So I won't deny any of what you said. But there's one thing more to be said, even so. Suppose we have only dreamed, or made up, all those things—trees and grass and sun and moon and stars and Aslan himself. Suppose we have. Then all I can say is that, in that case, the made-up things seem a good deal more important than the real ones. Suppose this black pit of a kingdom of yours is the only world. Well, it strikes me as a pretty poor one. And that's a funny thing, when you come to think of it. We're just babies making up a game, if you're right. But four babies playing a game can make a play-world which licks your real world hollow. That's why I'm going to stand by the play-world. I'm on Aslan's side even if there isn't any Aslan to lead it. I'm going to live as like a Narnian as I can even if there isn't any Narnia. So, thanking you kindly for our supper, if these two gentlemen and the young lady are ready, we're leaving your court at once and setting out in the dark to spend our lives looking for Overland. Not that our lives will be very long, I should think; but that's small loss if the world's as dull a place as you say." (*The Silver Chair*, Ch. 12)

Note three aspects of Puddleglum's response. First, Puddleglum's actual argument is a kind of *reductio ad absurdum*, a form of argument where you assume the opposite of what you're trying to prove in order to show that a logical contradiction follows. While Puddleglum doesn't demonstrate that the Witch's account of the world entails a *logical* contradiction, he does show that it at least entails a striking oddity, an improbability, even an absurdity. If the Witch's kingdom is all there is, then "four babies playing a game can make a play-world which licks your real world hollow" (Ch. 12). If the Witch is right, then the dreams of children are more beautiful, desirable, and attractive than anything in the black pit of reality.

This type of reasoning is related to one of Lewis's favorite arguments for the Christian faith: the argument from desire. A simple form of the argument appears in *Mere Christianity*.

> The Christian says, 'Creatures are not born with desires unless satisfaction for those desires exists. A baby feels hunger: well, there is such a thing as food. A duckling wants to swim: well, there is such a thing as water. Men feel sexual desire: well, there is such a thing as sex. If I find in myself a desire which no experience in this world can satisfy, the most probable explanation is that I was made for another world.[38]

In *Weight of Glory*, Lewis responds to a common objection to this argument, namely that the fact that we desire something doesn't prove that we will get it:

> Do what they will, then, we remain conscious of a desire which no natural happiness will satisfy. But is there any reason to suppose that reality offers any satisfaction to it? "Nor does the being hungry prove that we have bread." But I think it may be urged that this misses the point. A man's physical hunger does not prove that that man will get any bread; he may die of starvation on a raft in the Atlantic. But surely a man's hunger does prove that he comes of a race which repairs its body by eating and inhabits a world where eatable substances exist. In the same

way, though I do not believe (I wish I did) that my desire for Paradise proves that I shall enjoy it, I think it a pretty good indication that such a thing exists and that some men will. A man may love a woman and not win her; but it would be very odd if the phenomenon called "falling in love" occurred in a sexless world.[39]

In this light, Puddleglum's argument makes sense. In a world of darkness, desire for the sun is an oddity, a strange anomaly crying out for an explanation. In a world full of kittens, the desire for the strong comfort of a Good (though not Tame) Lion is stranger still. That such beautiful and attractive "fancies" would be invented by children is so outlandish, that the reasonable man (or Marshwiggle, as the case may be) is justified in rejecting the black pit and questing for Overland while living like a Narnian.

The second aspect of Puddleglum's response is the role of pain in producing it. This is no idle detail. Lewis really believed that pain, suffering, and hardship had a vital role in clearing the mind and enabling a person to see what really matters, and more importantly to hear from the One who speaks through the pain.

> We can ignore even pleasure. But pain insists upon being attended to. God whispers to us in our pleasures, speaks in our conscience, but shouts in our pains: it is his megaphone to rouse a deaf world.[40]

Finally, someone might think that Puddleglum's argument gives away too much, that it is essentially a blind leap in the dark, a willingness to believe any fable, however false, as long as it makes us feel warm and fuzzy inside. But Lewis rejects such rationalizations elsewhere in his writings. "If Christianity is untrue, then no honest man will want to believe it, however helpful it might be: if it is true, every honest man will want to believe it, even if it gives him no help at all."[41]

Since we know that Puddleglum is "an honest Marsh-wiggle" (Rilian called him one immediately before his speech), then we can safely conclude that he is not truly clinging to Aslan while actually agreeing with the Witch that it's all nonsense. Rather, he is providing a terrific example of how to remember in the dark what we have known in the light. Narnia is real, and Puddleglum had lived there his whole life. He really had seen a sky full of stars, and the sun coming up out of the sea in the morning, shining brightly in the midday sky, and then sinking behind the mountains at night. His faithful and obedient confession is no blind leap, but a deep commitment to his own experience of the truth of Overland, Narnia, and Aslan. In this way, Puddleglum is a model for all true Narnians (and all true Christians) and beautifully demonstrates the truth of Screwtape's words to his devilish nephew:

> Our cause is never more in danger than when a human, no longer desiring, but still intending, to do our Enemy's will, looks round upon a universe from which every trace of Him seems to have vanished, and asks why he has been forsaken, and still obeys.[42]

10

Shasta's Hard Lesson

Receiving the Reward for a Job Well Done

As a college professor in a small school whose core values include intentional mentorship and discipleship, I regularly find myself talking with students about their spiritual journey and their plans for the future. In listening to their struggles, a common refrain is the confusion that often sets in when a spiritually dry season follows a time of tremendous growth.

The basic story is remarkably consistent: God breaks in on them in a surprising and life-altering way and they begin to grow in grace by leaps and bounds. The Scriptures come alive in fresh and exciting ways as God begins to conform their souls to the image of his Son. Bible-reading and prayer are almost effortless, a great delight rather than a chore, and the pursuit of holiness is as natural as breathing.

Inevitably, the story takes a turn, leading them down into the valley of shadows. Spiritual vitality dries up, the zeal for the Scriptures and prayer is sapped of strength, and holiness begins to feel like Adam's work outside the garden, with the ground relentlessly fighting back against all efforts to cultivate it. It's at these points that they usually make their way to my office, looking for hope and help in recovering the joy of their salvation.

In almost all cases, the chief struggle is the same: *What have I done wrong that has landed me in this pit?* The contrast between the unbridled joy of their former experience and the frustrating doldrums of their present experience leads them to suppose that they must have committed some grievous sin which has caused God to remove his felt presence from them. The emotional dryness, the spiritual exhaustion, the numbness bordering on depression— surely these are signs of God's chastisement and displeasure.

A Painful and Perplexing Promotion

When faced with a student in such a state, I've found that some probing and fact-finding is in order. I first want to determine if they have in fact fallen into gross sin, in which case their heavy dryness is most likely God's disciplining work, and the proper remedy is found in confession and repentance. However, if what they're experiencing is primarily heightened temptation to sin and they find themselves struggling hard to resist it, and it is this increased struggle that is bound up with their present distress, then I generally return to the same wisdom that has encouraged me in similar situations.

I look across my desk at the confused and struggling student and say, "Congratulations. You've been promoted."

Which brings me to my favorite of the Narnian stories—*The Horse and His Boy*. It has become my favorite for a variety of reasons, some of which will become evident in subsequent chapters. But one key reason is that I find myself returning to it again and again in counseling and discipleship as a way of helping struggling Christians to press into the grace of God and continue to fight the good fight.

After my congratulations is met with a puzzled and slightly bewildered look, I then quote (or paraphrase) from memory the following passage from *The Horse and His Boy*:

> [Shasta] had not yet learned that if you do one good deed your reward usually is to be set to do another and harder and better one. (Ch. 10)

The New, Hard, and Better Task

In the story, Shasta and his friends have just travelled across the sweltering desert with little food, water, or rest. Their mission is to warn King Lune of Archenland of the imminent attack of Rabadash and his two hundred Calormene horsemen. After barely making it to the river in the gorge and collapsing in exhaustion, the four messengers (Shasta, Aravis, Bree, and Hwin) arise and discover that Rabadash is closer than they thought, and they find themselves in a race to King Lune.

In the midst of their gallop, a lion gives a snarling roar and begins to chase them, compounding their already difficult task with the fear of being eaten. As they're being chased, Shasta thinks to himself, "It's not fair. I *did* think we'd be safe from lions here." The lion closes in on Hwin and Aravis, and Shasta, in a moment of instinctive bravery, jumps off of Bree and runs weaponless at the lion, screaming, "Go home! Go home!" Surprisingly, his words have the desired effect, and the lion abandons his chase after wounding Aravis.

Shasta turns and races to the gate of the Hermit of the Southern March, where the horses and Aravis have collapsed in a heap of exhaustion. The Hermit helps the wounded Aravis down from her horse and then says to Shasta,

> And now, my son, waste no time on questions, but obey. This damsel is wounded. Your horses are spent. Rabadash is at this moment finding a

ford over the Winding Arrow. If you run now, without a moment's rest, you will still be in time to warn King Lune. (Ch. 10)

Shasta's reaction is the same as any of ours would have been. "Shasta's heart fainted at these words for he felt he had no strength left. And he writhed inside at what seemed the cruelty and unfairness of the demand." Nevertheless, he asks for directions to King Lune and then sets off running as fast as he can. It is in this way that he learned the painful lesson that the reward for obedience is to be given a new, harder, but better task.

Soaring, Running, and Walking for the Lion's Reward

This is the lesson I try to communicate to my students. Our mountaintop experiences of God and his grace are wonderful, and cause for gratitude and rejoicing. But God never leaves us on the mountaintop. Once we have been nourished and learned to obey in the sunlight of God's felt presence, surrounded by his hedge of protection, he then sends us outside the camp, into the wilderness, where the heat of temptation saps our strength and spiritual refreshment is hard to come by. Many travelers lose their way in the wilderness, stumbling into one pit or another.

The ones who make it are those who know deep in their bones that they ought not be surprised by such trials and temptations, as if something strange were happening to them. This is God's way, the way of the cross, and the proper response is to rejoice in the sufferings so that we may rejoice in the glory when it is revealed. We must learn the biblical lesson that God often sends lions to chase us so that we, like Bree, can discover that we weren't going quite as fast as we could. Like Shasta, we must learn to fall off the horse and "get up again without crying and mount again and fall again and yet not be afraid of falling" (Ch. 1).

Our lives are to be a long obedience in the same direction, and our direction is far more important than our pace. It's not unusual on this journey to grow faint and weary, even at times to stumble and fall. But hoping in the Lord, we can renew our strength and endeavor by grace to be faithful in little so that God will put us over much. In doing so, sometimes God allows us to take off like a rocket so that we soar like eagles, flying effortlessly above the hills and valleys on the ground. Other times we run, sometimes on the beaten path, sometimes off it, making good time while our spiritual legs and lungs are strengthened. Other times, we merely walk (or even crawl) in the direction that God has set for us. And in faithfully obeying even when it's hard, in pushing our spiritual muscles to their limit, in running with trembling limbs, a stitch in our side, and sweat in our eyes, we show ourselves to be true sons and daughters of Archenland and win from the Lion a great and happy reward.

11

A Society of Self-Regard

Learning to Whistle Like a Humble Narnian

Lewis is a master of communicating the feel of something using implicit, suggestive descriptions. He knows how to "describe around" something, allowing you to circle it through his words and get a sense of its contours and dimensions. This idea of a "sense," or intuitive impression, is what always comes to mind when I think about Calormene society.

Our first real introduction to the people of Calormen is in *The Voyage of the Dawn Treader*, where a few of them are engaged in the slave trade on the Lone Islands. They are described as a "wise, wealthy, courteous, cruel and ancient people" (*The Voyage of the Dawn Treader*, Ch. 4). They have a darker complexion than Narnians and Archenlanders, long beards which are sometimes dyed crimson, and they wear orange robes and turbans. The similarities to Middle-Eastern society are clearly intentional, and thus it's no surprise that their large empire is situated to the south of Narnia across a great desert.

Worship and the Calormene Culture

Some condemn Lewis for racism and ethnocentrism because of his unflattering depiction of Calormene/Middle-Eastern culture. Lewis certainly believes that cultures can be superior to each other, both in particular ways and in a cumulative, overall sense. What's more, he clearly depicts Narnian culture as both superior to Calormene culture on the whole and in terms of particular cultural expressions, such as the Narnian rejection of the slave trade and the happy liberty of Narnian society.

However, Narnian culture is not universally superior; Calormene story-telling outstrips its Narnian counterpart (even if Narnian poetry is more lively and compelling than that of Calormen), and the capital city of Tashbaan is "one of the wonders of the world." On top of that, Aravis in *The Horse and His Boy* and Emeth in *The Last Battle* both display Calormene virtues, even as they also deviate in significant ways from their fellow southerners. Finally, the roots of Narnian cultural superiority are not to be found in race or ethnicity, but in worship and allegiance.

For Lewis, underneath culture is *cultus*—worship—and if you worship a bloodthirsty and demonic god like Tash, then your culture will come to reflect him, just as if you worship a liberating and loving deity like Aslan, your culture will reflect him.

The Oppressive Structure of Calormene Society

My main interest in Calormene culture is the shape and structure of their social relationships. Like Narnia, Calormen society is divided into classes, with Tarkaans and Tarkheenas at the top and peasants, workers, and slaves at the bottom, with the Tisroc above all. This bears a structural similarity to the Narnian hierarchy of kings, lords and ladies of the court, and then the free Narnians. However, it's this last phrase that makes all the difference. In Narnia, those outside the royal court are considered freemen, and while they should honor their kings and lords, they are not their servants. The different Narnian classes mingle freely and recognize their common "humanity" (for lack of a better term), treating each other with mutual dignity and respect. In Calormen, the class structure is rigid, and lower classes are cut off from the Tisroc and his Tarkaans and relate to them more like slaves to masters (and not kind masters, but those who kick and cuff and call their slaves names their whole lives).

The layout of the city of Tashbaan testifies to this Calormene hierarchy, with the lower classes living in the lower terraces of the city amidst poverty, beggars, ragged children, hens, unwashed people, unwashed dogs, and piles of refuse. As one ascends the city streets, the houses become finer and more pleasant, with great statues, palm trees, green branches, cool fountains, and smooth lawns. At the top of the city is the palace of the Tisroc, a magnificent building full of great halls and terraces, and which one can only enter if you've been invited by the "palace-people" (*The Horse and His Boy*, Ch. 4).

More evidence for this Calormene class division is found in the use of litters as transportation by Tarkaans and Tarkheenas. These litters are carried by four to six gigantic slaves, who hoist them on their bare shoulders. What's more, in Tashbaan, "there is only one traffic regulation, which is that everyone who is less important has to get out of the way for everyone who is more important; unless you want a cut from a whip or punch from the butt end of a spear" (Ch. 4). Calormene rulers lord it over their subjects, demanding hospitality from them and then despising it when it's given. They also live in opulence and splendor—decked in pearls, bathing in milk, and spending their days at parties on the river.

The Tisroc is a cruel king who rules his subjects with a harsh hand. He condemns one of the cooks (to either prison or death) for causing some indigestion. His subjects are never allowed to turn their back to him. Even the Grand Vizier, his chief counselor and advisor, must grovel and address the Tisroc lying face down on the floor, subjecting himself to the ever-present threat of being kicked for no good reason. The Tisroc pays his wisdom an underhanded compliment, comparing it to "a costly jewel. . . . hidden in a dunghill" (Ch. 8).

Forced Flattery, False Affection, and Groveling Resentment

The results of this sharp class division are manifest. Resentment and anger are veiled beneath an appearance of affection. Prince Rabadash addresses his father as "Oh-my-father-and-oh-the-delight-of-my-eyes" but it is quite clear that he does not delight in his father at all. The feeling is apparently mutual, as the Tisroc is willing to send his eldest son on a risky mission that will likely end in his death, because, as he says, Rabadash is "beginning to be dangerous." There is no love lost between this father and son, as the following exchange makes clear:

> "If you were not my father, O ever-living Tisroc," said the Prince, grinding his teeth, "I should say that was the word of a coward."
>
> "And if you were not my son, O most inflammable Rabadash," replied his father, "your life would be short and your death slow when you had said it." (The cool, placid voice in which he spoke these words made Aravis's blood run cold.) (Ch. 8)

In addition to the forced flattery and veiled mistrust, the people of Calormene are very concerned with outward appearances and status. One detects a competitive jockeying for position through strategic marriages and the possibility of rising in the Tisroc's court. This is why Lasaraleen admires the Grand Vizier despite the fact that he is (according to Aravis) "a hideous groveling slave who flatters when he's kicked but treasures it all up and hopes to get his own back by egging on that horrible Tisroc to plot his son's death" (Ch. 9). It is very difficult to imagine genuine friendship developing in such a self-important, posturing, flattery-filled society.

Indeed, the Calormene society, if taken to its sinful extreme, would no doubt look very much like Lewis's description of Hell in the Preface to his book *The Screwtape Letters*: "We must picture Hell as a state where everyone is perpetually concerned about his own dignity and advancement, where everyone has a grievance, and where everyone lives the deadly serious passions of envy, self-importance, and resentment."[43]

The Ugly Effects of Breathing Calormene Air

An ugly picture indeed. But to see the real effects of Calormene society, we can consider Bree, the talking horse of Narnia who has been enslaved in Calormen his whole life. For Bree has breathed much Calormene air, and the effect upon him is more substantial than he knows.

For starters, he also is very concerned with his appearance and dignity. When Shasta says that Bree looks funny when he rolls on the ground for pleasure, the horse grows very anxious and worries that Narnian horses will look down on him for such a "silly, clownish trick" and "low, bad habits" (Ch. 2). Later, Bree, who is a great war-horse, is put off and offended when Hwin suggests that he should pretend to be a mere pack-horse. The thought of cutting his tail in order to escape detection greatly concerns him, since he doesn't want to arrive in Narnia with a disagreeable appearance. The closer they get to Narnia, the more nervous and self-conscious Bree becomes, since he is ignorant of Narnian customs and is sure to make dreadful mistakes. When they finally make it to Narnia, his overwhelming concern for his dignity and appearance leads him to look "more like a horse going to a funeral than a long-lost captive returning to home and freedom" (Ch. 14).

Additionally, Bree is a proud horse, boasting of his valor in battles and dismissing Hwin's attempt to press on despite their exhaustion by retorting, "I think, Ma'am," said Bree very crushingly, "that I know a little more about campaigns and forced marches and what a horse can stand than you do" (Ch. 9). For all his boasts, however, he proves to be susceptible to great fear, as evidenced by his own panicked conduct when the four travelers are chased by a lion. He is so ashamed that he mopes in the corner and announces that he will not be going to Narnia at all, but instead will return to Calormen.

> "Yes," said Bree. "Slavery is all I'm fit for. How can I ever show my face among the free Horses of Narnia?—I who left a mare and a girl and a boy to be eaten by lions while I galloped all I could to save my own wretched skin!. . . . I've lost everything." (Ch. 10)

However, beneath this show of humility, there is still a strong current of pride and self-regard, which rises up as soon as the Hermit rebukes him:

> My good Horse, you've lost nothing but your self-conceit. No, no, cousin. Don't put back your ears and shake your mane at me. If you are really so humbled as you sounded a minute ago, you must learn to listen to sense. You're not quite the great Horse you had come to think, from living among poor dumb horses. Of course you were braver and cleverer than them. You could hardly help being that. It doesn't follow that you'll be anyone very special in Narnia. But as long as you know you're nobody very special, you'll be a very decent sort of Horse, on the whole, and taking one thing with another. (Ch. 10)

Searching for Self-Regard Through Self-Examination

This picture of Calormene society and its effects on people (and horses) should lead us to ask some probing questions about ourselves, our families, our churches, and our communities. For example:

- Are we overly concerned with appearances and status? Do we find ourselves always jockeying for position and competing with others for the highest place?

- When in authority, do we lord it over our subordinates, demanding that they serve us and treating them with contempt?
- Are our expressions of affection genuine or simply a show to impress others? Beneath our words and actions, is there seething resentment or grasping envy or deceitful malice?
- Do we engage in vain flattery of others as a way of manipulating them? Are our compliments and encouragements sincere?
- Are we overly concerned with our own dignity, seeking compliments in order to massage our egos? Do we draw attention to our own gifts and accomplishments as a way of eliciting praise from others?
- And, when we are brought low by our sin, is our humility real or merely external? How would we respond if we confessed to someone, "I am the chief of sinners" and they agreed with us? Would we put our ears back, bow our neck, and shake our mane?

From Haughty Self-Regard to Humble Self-Forgetfulness

No doubt other questions could be asked. But I want to close this chapter by reflecting on the alternative to such pride, self-regard, and the closed and ugly society that results. C. S. Lewis understood humility perhaps better than any other modern author, and his books are littered with profound descriptions of this fundamental Christian virtue. The following passage from *Mere Christianity* tackles Calormene society head on.

We must not think Pride is something God forbids because He is offended at it, or that Humility is something He demands as due to His own dignity—as if God Himself was proud. He is not in the least worried about His dignity. The point is, He wants you to know Him: wants to give you Himself. And He and you are two things of such a kind that if you really get into any kind of touch with Him you will, in fact, be humble—delightedly humble, feeling the infinite relief of having for once got rid of all the silly nonsense about your own dignity which has made you restless and unhappy all your life. He is trying to make you humble in order to make this moment possible: trying to take off a lot of silly, ugly, fancy-dress in which we have all got ourselves up and are strutting about like the little idiots we are. I wish I had got a bit further with humility myself: if I had, I could probably tell you more about the relief, the comfort, of taking the fancy-dress off—getting rid of the false self, with all its 'Look at me' and 'Aren't I a good boy?' and all its posing and posturing. To get even near it, even for a moment, is like a drink of cold water to a man in a desert.[44]

To be truly humble is to dispense with the silly nonsense about our own dignity, all the posing and posturing. We are to put off our Calormene pride (what Paul calls 'the old man') in order to put on Narnian humility, which does not look at all like the groveling lowliness of the Grand Vizier.

Do not imagine that if you meet a really humble man he will be what most people call 'humble' nowadays: he will not be a sort of greasy, smarmy person, who is always telling you that, of course, he is nobody. Probably all you will think about him is that he seemed a cheerful, intelligent chap who took a real interest in what you said to him. If you do dislike him it will be because you feel a little envious of anyone who seems to enjoy life so easily. He will not be thinking about humility: he will not be thinking about himself at all.[45]

Breathing Narnian Air

This glorious self-forgetfulness finds expression in the wonderful passage in *The Horse and His Boy* in which Shasta sees the Narnians for the first time on the streets of Tashbaan. Breathing the air of this passage has deeply shaped the kind of person I want to be, providing me with a vision of living like a Narnian in the freedom and beauty of true humility and self-forgetfulness. I offer it here without comment, and commend it to you for your reflection and meditation.

And there was no litter; everyone was on foot. There were about half a dozen men and Shasta had never seen anyone like them before. For one thing, they were all as fair-skinned as himself, and most of them had fair hair. And they were not dressed like men of Calormen. Most of them had legs bare to the knee. Their tunics were of fine, bright, hardy colors—woodland green, or gay yellow, or fresh blue. Instead of turbans they wore steel or silver caps, some of them set with jewels, and one with little wings on each side. A few were bare-headed. The swords at their sides were long and straight, not curved like Calormene scimitars. And instead of being grave and mysterious like most Calormenes, they walked with a swing and let their arms and shoulders go free, and chatted and laughed. One was whistling. You could see that they were ready to be friends with anyone who was friendly and didn't give a fig for anyone who wasn't. Shasta thought he had never seen anything so lovely in his life. (Ch. 4)

12

The Heart of the Laughing King

Learning from Lune What It Means to Be a Man

My favorite character in all of the Narnian stories is King Lune of Archenland. This may seem odd, given that he is only a minor character, and he only appears in one story, and only for a few scenes in the last third of it. Nevertheless, his words, actions, and overall demeanor have had a profound impact on me, one that only increases as I grow older.

King Lune is described as "the jolliest, fat, apple-cheeked, twinkling-eyed King you could imagine." Elsewhere, he is identified as "the kindest hearted of men," willing to let go of his anger toward the evil and bombastic Rabadash after Aslan turns the Calormene prince into a donkey.

A Beautiful Picture of True Manhood

Lune is a man under authority, gladly embracing the truth that "the king's under the law, for it's the law makes him king. Hast no more

power to start away from thy crown than any sentry from his post"
(*The Horse and His Boy*, Ch. 15). He has no pretensions of being
"the Boss," but willingly submits himself to a Higher Authority.

He is a master of propriety and tact, able to model appropriate
behavior in a wide array of situations. He shows himself to be both
a dignified king, who gives Aravis a stately bow and kind words of
welcome, and a man who is willing to get his hands dirty cleaning
the kennels of his hunting dogs.

He is a valiant and capable warrior, defeating the Tarkaan
Azrooh in hand-to-hand combat. Yet he is also tender-hearted and
merciful, unwilling to execute traitors in cold blood, even those
who would have gladly murdered every male within his walls,
down to the baby that was born yesterday.

He is thick-skinned and stable, not prone to rage or fits, maintaining his composure and sense of decorum even when grossly
insulted by Rabadash in his court. He even rebukes his lords for
allowing themselves to be provoked and shaken by the "taunt of a
pajock." Moreover, he chastises his youngest son for mocking the
defeated and imprisoned prince, saying "Never taunt a man save
when he is stronger than you: then, as you please" (Ch. 15). In other
words, even mockery has its proper place, provided you are the sole
faithful prophet on the mountain, surrounded by 400 prophets of
Baal who are making fools of themselves before their false gods.

A Father of Manifest Delight

Beyond his faithfulness, wisdom, and tact as king, Lune is a remarkable father, modeling the right mix of toughness and tenderness for his boys. As we've seen, he's willing to rebuke his son on
occasion and teach him what it means to be a man. He chides
Corin for his disobedience, even though he is genuinely proud of
him for his bravery and valor in battle (Ch. 13).

Just as important, if not more so, is his evident and manifest
delight in his sons. When he sees them, his face lights up and he

holds out his arms to greet them. His face noticeably brightens with fatherly pride when he hears how Shasta courageously rescued Aravis from the lion. And when it is revealed that Shasta is in fact Cor, the king's oldest son, the young fatherless boy finds himself "suddenly embraced in a bear-like hug by King Lune and kissed on both cheeks" (Ch. 13). In short, Lune beautifully shows what it means to be an affectionate father who is well-pleased with his beloved sons, so much so that even after a few days with him Shasta can say, "Father's an absolute brick. I'd be just as pleased—or very nearly—at finding he's my father even if he wasn't a king" (Ch. 14).

King Lune is thus a fitting representative of Aslan's ideal of kingship, the ideal which the Great Lion expressed to King Frank, the first king of Narnia in *The Magician's Nephew* (Ch. 11). There Aslan describes a true king as one who works the ground to raise food out of the earth (and thus isn't above manual labor, but willing to get his hands dirty), rules kindly and fairly, not showing favoritism to anyone (either his sons or his lords), protects the land from enemies (like vicious Calormene princes), being the first in the charge and last in retreat, and trains his sons and grandsons to do the same (both by his example and by his words).

First In, Last Out, Laughing Loudest

Lune himself echoes these words in what may be my favorite passage in all of the Chronicles, a passage which awakens a deep yearning in my heart to be this kind of husband, this kind of father, this kind of man:

> For this is what it means to be a king: to be first in every desperate attack and last in every desperate retreat, and when there's hunger in the land (as must be now and then in bad years) to wear finer clothes and laugh louder over a scantier meal than any man in your land. (Ch. 15)

These are no mere words for the king. When the gates of Anvard open during the battle with Rabadash, King Lune is the first one out to face the foe. He knows deep in his heart that to be a leader means that you have the privilege of dying first. Kingship and headship, as both Aslan and Jesus have shown us, is about love and sacrifice, giving up your whole self for the sake of those in your care, even unto death.

Lune is a man familiar with grief and suffering, having lost a child and a wife at some point in the past. Despite these tragic losses, which, based on his clear affection for his loved ones, no doubt left a gaping hole in the great king's heart, the king is not eaten up by bitterness or resentment or grief. He is still jovial, still kind, still wise and judicious, still active and alert, still bright-eyed and thick-skinned.

For me, King Lune is a model, a wonderful picture of what it means to be a Narnian king, and therefore what it means to be a Christian man. I find myself often quoting his kingly description when speaking to college men who are trying to discover God's call on their lives. I can easily bring myself to tears thinking about my own sons, and how much I long to be for them—and therefore long for them to be—a man like King Lune of Archenland: stable and secure, sacrificial and giving, brave and valiant, big-hearted and great-souled, a man who has known grief, but with the deep confidence of one whose feet are firmly planted on a rock, still laughs at the time to come.

13

Tell Me Your Sorrows

Pursuing Healing through Happy Endings

As a father of young boys, one of the most moving passages in the Chronicles is found in Chapter 11 of *The Horse and His Boy*.

Shasta, Aravis, and the two horses have come across the desert bearing the warning for King Lune. The lion has chased them and wounded Aravis, and Shasta has learned the hard lesson that the reward for obedience is to be given another, more difficult task. He has run over hill and dale, found King Lune and his hunting party, and warned him of the imminent attack by Rabadash. As the Archenlanders race back to their castle, Shasta falls behind because he doesn't truly know how to ride and direct a horse. He's then forced off the road by Rabadash's cavalry and realizes that he can't make it to Anvard with the Calormene army between him and the castle. So he takes the other fork in the road and simply starts down it in hopes of finding some place to rest and eat.

As he rides up a mountain pass, a thick fog descends and Shasta begins to think about all of the hardships and difficulties that he's faced.

"I do think," said Shasta, "that I must be the most unfortunate boy that ever lived in the whole world. Everything goes right for everyone except me. Those Narnian lords and ladies got safe away from Tashbaan; I was left behind. Aravis and Bree and Hwin are all as snug as anything with that old Hermit: of course I was the one who was sent on. King Lune and his people must have got safely into the castle and shut the gates long before Rabadash arrived, but I get left out." (*The Horse and His Boy*, Ch. 11)

The combination of loneliness, exhaustion, and hunger overwhelms the poor boy, and he begins to cry so much that "the tears rolled down his cheeks."

When a Hard Life Gets Harder

There's no question but that Shasta has had a hard life. Taken from his true parents at a very young age, he is raised by a Calormene fisherman with an erratic temper who would box his ears for no good reason and treated him no better than a slave (Ch. 1). Living in the south of Calormen, he has no friends, no real companionship, just a lonely life filled with a deep yearning for something more, something over the hills to the North. He is effectively an orphan, with no education, no real love for his adoptive "father," and no hope for the future.

His escape to the North has been fraught with perils—roaring lions, the ever-present threat of being caught and executed as a horse-thief, the separation from his friends in Tashbaan, the fearful night at the tombs surrounded by howling jackals. What's more, every glimmer of hope seems to have been disappointed: he's taken in by the kind and caring Narnians, only to be forced to leave when Prince Corin returns. He arrives at the Hermit's house only to be told that he must not rest, but instead run, run, run. He meets King Lune and company only to lose them on the journey back. For his entire life Shasta has been at the mercy of forces beyond his control, tossed about by events and circumstances, cut off from love, affection, and security. Thinking about his lot is enough to make anyone tear up.

And then, to top it off, as he journeys down the road with a growling stomach and tired and tear-filled eyes, Something begins to walk along next to him, breathing deep sighs and filling Shasta with terror. He rides along with the Large Thing breathing beside him until he finally can't stand it any longer. In the dark he whispers, "Who are you?"

The Fear of Losing Mom

Now, let us leave Shasta for a moment and reflect upon the story of another young boy who has known hardship. In *The Magician's Nephew*, we first meet the young Digory Kirke after he's been crying over his own sorrows. His father is traveling far away in India, and he has been forced to live with his aunt and uncle (the latter of whom may very well be mad). Most importantly, his Mother, whom he loves very much, is very ill and is likely going to die.

Indeed, Digory's love for his Mother and desire for her health is a dominant and recurring feature of *The Magician's Nephew*. Uncle Andrew uses it to keep Digory from screaming when the old man deceives Polly and sends her to the Other World. When Jadis the Queen escapes into our world, Digory worries that the evil Witch will go into his Mother's room and "frighten her to death." In fact, Digory is more concerned about Jadis rampaging about the house and upsetting his Mother than he is about the Witch Queen tearing London apart with her bare hands (*The Magician's Nephew*, Ch. 6).

More than this, as the story progresses, Digory begins to hope against hope that he might be able to find a cure for his Mother in one of the Other Worlds, perhaps some magical fruit from the Land of Youth that will restore her health. The thought of "Mother well again" almost consumes him, filling him with the kind of hope that you fight against because it's too good to be true and you've been disappointed so often before (Ch. 7). But when Uncle Andrew describes the new land of Narnia as the land of youth, Digory's heart leaps and "that sweet hope rushed back upon him." He immediately seeks an audience with Aslan—though it takes a while for him to actually meet him—in order to ask for something, anything to cure his Mother. He is devastated when he realizes that he has unleashed the evil Witch upon Narnia, because he is sure that there is no way that Aslan will cure his Mother now (Ch. 11).

Echoes of Lewis in Digory and Shasta

Before showing how Lewis resolves the stories of both of these grief-stricken boys, it's worth dwelling on Lewis's own childhood for echoes of Shasta and Digory. For Lewis's childhood, while filled in some ways with idyllic joys and active imagination, also contains deep sorrow and sadness, the kind driven by the painful loss of a mother, and, in a sense, of a father. His autobiography, *Surprised by Joy*, describes his own recollections of his mother's death and his father's subsequent detachment, recollections that have deep resonances with the Narnian stories.

> There came a night when I was ill and crying both with headache and toothache and distressed because my mother did not come to me. That was because she was ill too; and what was odd was that there were several doctors in her room, and voices and comings and goings all over the house and doors shutting and opening. It seemed to last for hours. And then my father, in tears, came into my room and began to try to convey to my terrified mind things it had never conceived before. It was in fact cancer and followed the usual course; an operation (they operated in the patient's house in those days), an apparent convalescence, a return of the disease, increasing pain, and death. My father never fully recovered from this loss.[46]

Note the nine-year old Lewis's distress at his mother's absence in the midst of his own sickness, then the confusion of a house full of doctors, then the terrifying conversation with his father about the inconceivable loss that lay before them. In a later passage, he describes how he and his brother truly lost their mother before she died, as "she was gradually withdrawn from our life into the hands of nurses and delirium and morphia, and as our whole existence changed into something alien and menacing, as the house became full of strange smells and midnight noises and sinister whispered conversations."[47] This last comment recalls Digory's eavesdropping on the hushed conversations of doctors and housekeepers, and the peculiar kind of childhood terror that is created by adult agitation. Lewis goes on to remark that "the sight of adult misery and adult terror has an effect on children which is merely paralyzing and alienating."

It was during this season that Lewis offered the first prayers of his life: the desperate—and unanswered—prayers of a little child who doesn't want his mom to die. Finally, of course, Lewis laments not only the painful death of his mother, but the emotional loss of his father, which Lewis describes in this way:

> [My father's] nerves had never been of the steadiest and his emotions had always been uncontrolled. Under the pressure of anxiety his temper became incalculable; he spoke wildly and acted unjustly. Thus by a peculiar cruelty of fate, during those months the unfortunate man, had he but known it, was really losing his sons as well as his wife. We were coming, my brother and I, to rely more and more exclusively on each other for all that made life bearable; to have confidence only in each other. I expect that we (or at any rate I) were already learning to lie to him. Everything that had made the house a home had failed us; everything except one another. We drew daily closer together (that was the good result)—two frightened urchins huddled for warmth in a bleak world.[48]

His father's erratic temper, his injustice and lack of self-control, the resulting alienation from his sons—all of these find a partial echo in Shasta's hard relationship with his adoptive and abusive father Arsheesh. For both Shasta and Digory (like Lewis), "everything that had made the house a home had failed," leaving both boys desperate, lost, abandoned, and in tears.

And this is where we find them—two frightened urchins huddled for warmth in a bleak world, but now huddled in the presence of a Great Lion who is about to change their stories forever.

The Shining Tears of the Great Lion

With the hope of a cure for his Mother seemingly dashed, Digory is surprised when Aslan asks if he is ready to restore what his own foolishness had broken. He agrees to do so,

> But when he had said "Yes," he thought of his Mother, and he thought of the great hopes he had had, and how they were all dying away, and a lump came in his throat and tears in his eyes, and he blurted out: "But please, please—won't you—can't you give me something that will cure Mother?" (*The Magician's Nephew*, Ch. 12)

In this moment of childlike desperation, Digory asks for the impossible and then looks up into the Lion's face. "What he saw surprised him as much as anything in his whole life."

> For the tawny face was bent down near his own and (wonder of wonders) great shining tears stood in the Lion's eyes. They were such big, bright tears compared with Digory's own that for a moment he felt as if the Lion must really be sorrier about his Mother than he was himself.

"My son, my son," said Aslan. "I know. Grief is great. Only you and I in this land know that yet. Let us be good to one another." (Ch. 12)

Aslan knows. He knows pain. He knows sadness, anguish, and

loss. He is a Lion of Sorrows, acquainted with grief. And he so iden-tifies with the weakness and suffering of a lost, little boy that tears well up in his eyes and, in a moment of glorious condescension he stoops to give Digory a Lion's kiss.

That deep connection, that profound identification, those great, shared and shining tears sustain Digory when he is tempted to disobey the Lion's orders in retrieving the Apple of Youth from the Tree in the West. Upon his return with the Apple, Digory receives not only the Lion's "Well done!" but also an apple from the Protec-tive Tree, an apple that promises to make his Mother whole again. When she eats the apple, she immediately smiles and sinks into "a real, natural, gentle sleep." The doctor pronounces her recovery a miracle, and things only get better from there.

> About a week after this it was quite certain that Digory's Mother was getting better. About a fortnight later she was able to sit out in the gar-den. And a month later that whole house had become a different place. Aunt Letty did everything that Mother liked; windows were opened, frowsy curtains were drawn back to brighten up the rooms, there were new flowers everywhere, and nicer things to eat, and the old piano was tuned and Mother took up her singing again, and had such games with Digory and Polly that Aunt Letty would say "I declare, Mabel, you're the biggest baby of the three." (Ch. 15)

Digory's story ends (at least for now) with a hard, but good obedi-ence, a healthy mother, a returned father, a big, happy country house, and the glad approval of the Great Lion.

Shasta and the Triune Lion

Returning then to Shasta, we left him on his horse, riding in terror with a large, breathing and sighing Thing at his side, whispering a frightened question in the dark, "Who are you?"

"One who has waited long for you to speak," said the Thing. Its voice was not loud, but very large and deep.

"Are you—are you a giant?" asked Shasta.

"You might call me a giant," said the Large Voice. "But I am not like the creatures you call giants."

"I can't see you at all," said Shasta, after staring very hard. Then (for an even more terrible idea had come into his head) he said, almost in a scream, "You're not—not something dead, are you? Oh please—please do go away. What harm have I ever done you? Oh, I am the unluckiest person in the whole world!" (*The Horse and His Boy*, Ch. 11)

Then the Voice breathes a warm, reassuring breath on the frightened child and says, "Tell me your sorrows."

And Shasta does—from being orphaned and beaten by his adoptive father, to fleeing from multiple lions and hiding in ghoulish tombs, to the heat and thirst of the desert, and the loneliness and hunger of the present moment. For a boy who had never known true affection, for a boy who had bottled up all of the pain and loneliness in his heart, the opportunity to unload his cares, to unburden his soul, to be really and truly *heard* must have felt like a profound relief.

And then the Voice surprises him by saying, "I do not call you unfortunate," and then informs him that in all of his journeys, there was only one lion, "but he was swift of foot." And then, most shockingly of all, the Voice says, "I was the lion who forced you to join with Aravis. I was the cat who comforted you among the houses of the dead. I was the lion who drove the jackals from you while you slept. I was the lion who gave the Horses the new strength of fear for the last mile so that you should reach King Lune in time. And I was the lion you do not remember who pushed the boat in which you lay, a child near death, so that it came to shore where a man sat, wakeful at midnight, to receive you" (Ch. 11).

In this moment, Shasta discovers that behind a frowning providence, Aslan hides a smiling face. All that he had called "bad luck" and "misfortune" was really the wise and good plan of the Great Lion. As he says to Aravis later, Aslan "seems to be at the back of all the stories." Having come face to face with the One who has guided his every step, he presses to know more.

"Who are you?" asked Shasta.

"Myself," said the Voice, very deep and low so that the earth shook: and again "Myself," loud and clear and gay: and then the third time "Myself," whispered so softly you could hardly hear it, and yet it seemed to come from all round you as if the leaves rustled with it. (Ch. 11)

Aslan's triune identification is one of the more explicit Christian expressions in the Chronicles. It produces in Shasta a "new and different sort of trembling," mingled with gladness and hope that the night was over at last. Seeing the face of the terrible, beautiful, and shining Lion, Shasta slips out of the saddle and falls at his feet. "He couldn't say anything but then he didn't want to say anything, and he knew he needn't say anything" (Ch. 11).

Having met the triune Lion face to face, Shasta's life is forever changed. For not only has he come to know the King above all High Kings in Narnia, but he is soon reunited with his real father, Lune of Archenland, the kind and big-hearted king with a twinkle in his eye and deep affection for his son.

Imagination, Wish-Fulfillment, and Deep Comfort

Given the similarity of Lewis's own story with Digory's and Shasta's—with the key difference being Mother's recovery and the reunion with a loving father—someone (perhaps a Freudian?) might object that Lewis is simply engaged in a kind of wish-fulfillment and escapist therapy, working through his childhood pain by re-writing his own story with a happy ending. I, for one, can imagine Lewis replying,

Perhaps I am working through my own pain and loss through these stories. But what of it? We live in a world in which mothers die. Might we not imagine a world in which they are well again? Fathers can be harsh and intemperate. Can we not for a moment picture them as jovial and affectionate? Or have we grown too cynical to hope? And might the real answer to such childhood pain lie elsewhere? Isn't the true import of Shasta and Digory found in their willingness to forego second things (however precious) in favor of things of first importance? Don't their stories really demonstrate how crucial it is to put first things first (even if in the end, they also have second things thrown in)? Indeed, might the real comfort, the deep comfort come, not from the restoration of a mother's health, or the recovery of a happy father, but in the shining tears and smiling face of the High King above all kings?

14

A High and Lonely Destiny

The Dangerous Trajectory of Those Who Seek to Be Gods

Reading Lewis today, it's easy to believe that he was a prophet (or at least the son of a prophet). His analysis of education, government, culture, society, and the church has proved to be unusually prescient. One of the chief reasons for this is that Lewis understood the deep reality of narrative, of story, of progression and trajectory. This is something that many today, for all of our talk of Christian worldview, do not truly grasp—or at least, if we grasp it, we don't always apply it with the level of insight that he does.

In Chapter 3, I showed how in Edmund's character Lewis communicates to us the profound truth that we are all headed somewhere and sooner or later, we're bound to arrive. We may not like our destination, but that is neither here nor there. We have all boarded the train, and it is inexorably going somewhere. This is what Douglas Wilson calls an inescapable question: It is not whether we will have a destination, but which destination we will have. Not whether we will choose to go, but where.

Lewis is capable of portraying this truth through a single character, or, as in *The Magician's Nephew*, through a comparison of a few characters. As we read about Uncle Andrew, Jadis, and Digory, we are meant to see something crucial, not only for us as individuals, but for our communities and indeed the world as a whole.

The Tyranny of Scientific Conditioners

Before reflecting on these characters, it's worth reminding ourselves of some things that Lewis writes about in *The Abolition of Man*. There Lewis argues that men who have rejected the *Tao* (that is, traditional morality, the wisdom of the ages, the God-given order of the universe) have substituted for it the desire to conquer Nature through science and technology. A number of results follow from this.

First, "what we call Man's power over Nature turns out to be a power exercised by some men over other men with Nature as its instrument."[49] Because we are aiming to conquer Nature through science and technology, those who possess the technology have the power and ability to give or withhold it from the rest of mankind. In this way, "Man's conquest of Nature, if the dreams of some scientific planners are realized, means the rule of a few hundreds of men over billions upon billions of men."[50]

Second, because the conquest of Nature includes the attempted modification of *human* nature, such an endeavor truly means Nature's conquest of Man, that is, the reduction of Man to an "artefact," an object, or, in other words, the turning of Man into a "thing"—a *He* into an *it*. The scientific planners primarily engaged in this conquest are therefore compelled by a lust for power, the desire to control and shape the destinies of the rest of humanity (this is why Lewis refers to them as "the Conditioners").

Third, in order to modify Man, these Conditioners must begin to "use" particular men as test subjects and guinea pigs. To do this, they must set aside their shared humanity and reject the common

Law which stands over all men (namely, the *Tao*). As Lewis says, "the conditioners have been emancipated from all that. . . . They themselves are outside, above." In seeking to be gods, they have ceased to be men, at least men in the traditional sense. They are, in essence, Former Men, "men who have sacrificed their own share in traditional humanity in order to devote themselves to the task of deciding what 'Humanity' shall henceforth mean."[51]

Fourth, the last quotation introduces the key element of Time into the picture. For the tyranny of the Conditioners extends beyond their own generation. Indeed, one of their fundamental motivations is to shape what Man shall be in the future.

> In order to understand fully what Man's power over Nature, and therefore the power of some men over other men, really means, we must picture the race extended in time from the date of its emergence to that of its extinction. Each generation exercises power over its successors: and each, in so far as it modifies the environment bequeathed to it and rebels against tradition, resists and limits the power of its predecessors.[52]

Finally, it's worth highlighting the historical connection Lewis draws between the scientist's quest for power and the magician's lust for the same.

> I have described as a 'magician's bargain' that process whereby man surrenders object after object, and finally himself, to Nature in return for power. And I meant what I said. The fact that the scientist has succeeded where the magician failed has put such a wide contrast between them in popular thought that the real story of the birth of Science is misunderstood. You will even find people who write about the sixteenth century as if Magic were a medieval survival and Science the new thing that came in to sweep it away. Those who have studied the period know better. There was very little magic in the Middle Ages: the sixteenth and seventeenth centuries are the high noon of magic. The serious magical

endeavour and the serious scientific endeavour are twins: one was sickly and died, the other strong and throve. But they were twins. They were born of the same impulse.[53]

Later he writes,

There is something which unites magic and applied science while separating both from the 'wisdom' of earlier ages. For the wise men of old the cardinal problem had been how to conform the soul to reality, and the solution had been knowledge, self-discipline, and virtue. For magic and applied science alike the problem is how to subdue reality to the wishes of men: the solution is a technique; and both, in the practice of this technique, are ready to do things hitherto regarded as disgusting and impious—such as digging up and mutilating the dead.[54]

The Queen and the Magician: Using People and Craving Power

With this background, we're now in a position to compare Uncle Andrew, Jadis, and Digory. We begin with the first two. It is clear that Lewis intends us to see a family resemblance between the Magician and the Queen. Polly recognized "a sort of likeness between her face and his, something in the expression," which the narrator identifies as the "Mark" that all wicked Magicians have (*The Magician's Nephew*, Ch. 6). Both of them are described as having a "hungry and greedy look" when they think about exercising power over others. They both gain power at some significant cost to themselves. Andrew had to get to know "some devilish queer people, and go through some very disagreeable experiences" (Ch. 2). Jadis pays "a terrible price" to learn the Deplorable Word (Ch. 5).

The deepest resemblance between the two is their utter devotion to power and their complete disregard for others, except when they want to use people in pursuit of more power. When Digory expresses concern for Polly after Uncle Andrew sends her out of the world, the magician responds, "How you do harp on that! As if that was what mattered." He chastises Digory for "getting off the point" when Digory objects to the use of guinea-pigs as test subjects. When Digory calls him a coward for sending a little girl somewhere that he was afraid to go, Uncle Andrew erupts in a flurry of bombast.

> Silence, sir! I am the great scholar, the magician, the adept, who is doing the experiment. Of course I need subjects to do it on. Bless my soul, you'll be telling me next that I ought to have asked the guinea-pigs' permission before I used them! No great wisdom can be reached without sacrifice. But the idea of my going myself is ridiculous. It's like asking a general to fight as a common soldier. Supposing I got killed, what would become of my life's work? (Ch. 2)

Likewise Jadis only takes notice of people when she wants to use them, ignoring Polly when she wants to use Digory, and then ignoring both children in order to use Uncle Andrew. When Digory and Polly express shock that she would kill every living thing on Charn (including ordinary people, women, children, and animals) in order to prevent her sister from gaining power, Jadis issues a chilling reply.

> "Don't you understand?" said the Queen (still speaking to Digory). "I was the Queen. They were all my people. What else were they there for but to do my will?" (Ch. 5)

As in *The Abolition of Man*, Lewis intends for us to connect this willingness to callously use people and animals with modern science as practiced by Conditioners. Both the Witch and the Magician are described as "dreadfully practical," uninterested in things or people "unless they can use them." Uncle Andrew repeatedly identifies his work as "a great experiment," likening it to scientific endeavors.

Bursting the Bonds of Ordinary Morality

Lewis solidifies this connection between Jadis and Uncle Andrew (and between them and the Conditioners) by putting identical words in each character's mouth. When Digory calls his uncle "rotten" for failing to keep his promises, Uncle Andrew gives the following patronizing response.

> "Rotten?" said Uncle Andrew with a puzzled look. "Oh, I see. You mean that little boys ought to keep their promises. Very true: most right and proper, I'm sure, and I'm very glad you have been taught to do it. But of course you must understand that rules of that sort, however excellent they may be for little boys—and servants—and women—and even people in general, can't possibly be expected to apply to profound students and great thinkers and sages. No, Digory. Men like me, who possess hidden wisdom, are freed from common rules just as we are cut off from common pleasures. Ours, my boy, is a high and lonely destiny." (Ch. 2)

Jadis expresses an identical sentiment when Digory sympathizes with the common people of Charn who are killed when the Queen utters the Deplorable Word.

> I had forgotten that you are only a common boy. How should you understand reasons of State? You must learn, child, that what would be wrong for you or for any of the common people is not wrong in a great Queen such as I. The weight of the world is on our shoulders. We must be freed from all rules. Ours is a high and lonely destiny. (Ch. 5)

In both cases, the Magicians (like the Conditioners) are above ordinary morality. They are set off from common people so that the rules and laws of the *Tao* do not apply to them. However, despite being outside of the *Tao*, both Jadis and Uncle Andrew are willing to falsely imitate it in order to manipulate the children. Uncle Andrew uses flattering compliments, feigned generosity, and expressions of love in order to deceive Polly into touching a yellow ring (Ch. 1). Jadis tempts Digory to disobey Aslan and steal an apple by pretending to be deeply concerned for the health of his sick Mother (Ch. 13). Additionally, Uncle Andrew attempts to hold the values and expectations of the *Tao* over Digory's head, appealing to honor and chivalry and his friendship with Polly and chiding him for his disobedience and impertinence, all in order to get the boy to do what he wants.

With the deep resemblance between Uncle Andrew and Jadis established, we must also recognize the profound difference between them. Put simply, Jadis shows the lust for power taken to an extreme, while Andrew embodies a milder form of tyranny and the rejection of the *Tao*. Jadis demonstrates the extent of her wickedness in the ease with which she describes the layout of her palace on Charn.

> "That is the door to the dungeons," she would say, or "That passage leads to the principal torture chambers," or "This was the old banqueting hall where my great-grandfather bade seven hundred nobles to a feast and killed them all before they had drunk their fill. They had had rebellious thoughts." (Ch. 5)

While Andrew may dislike ordinary people and experiment on children and guinea pigs, he is not yet capable of destroying entire worlds for the sake of his power. What's more, he is clearly out of his league when it comes to Magic, demonstrating a dangerous ignorance of what it can do. Lewis, with perhaps a rye look at modern scientists, remarks, "Uncle Andrew, you see, was working with things he did not really understand; most magicians are" (Ch. 3).

That we are to see a progression from Andrew to Jadis is confirmed by the faces of the figures in Charn's Hall of Images (Ch. 4). The oldest faces are "kind and wise" (Jadis later describes them as "soft-hearted" and unwilling to search for the Deplorable Word). As you make your way down the row, they steadily become "solemn" and strict ("You felt you would have to mind your P's and Q's, if you ever met living people who looked like that"). By the middle of the room, the faces are "very strong and proud and happy," but also cruel. Moving forward, the faces grow crueler, losing their happiness and gaining despair "as if the people they belonged to had done dreadful things and also suffered dreadful things." The final figure, of course, is Jadis herself, the Last Queen of Charn, who blotted out that world forever. This world-ending generational trajectory mirrors Lewis's warning about the conquest of Nature and the tyranny of the Conditioners. And it is on this slope that Digory is in danger of slipping.

Sowing Seeds of the Lust for Power

In Digory, we can see the lust for power and the rejection of the Tao in seed form. The narrator describes him as "the sort of person who wants to know everything." When Polly is unnerved by Charn and wants to return home, Digory insists on having a look around, manipulatively implying that Polly is needlessly afraid. In the Hall of Images, he goes "wild with curiosity," longing to know the words on the pillar and then convincing himself that he is under their spell. When Polly calls him on his foolishness, he dismisses her by saying, "It's because you're a girl. Girls never want to know anything but gossip and rot about people getting engaged" (you couldn't find a finer example of the fallacy of Bulverism[55]). The subsequent back and forth between the two is damning:

> "You looked exactly like your Uncle when you said that," said Polly.
>
> "Why can't you keep to the point?" said Digory. "What we're talking about is—"
>
> "How exactly like a man!" said Polly in a very grown-up voice. (Ch. 4)

More than just looking like his Uncle, Digory is beginning to behave like him. Earlier in the story, Uncle Andrew had similarly dismissed Digory's warning by saying, "Well, well, I suppose that is a natural thing for a child to think—brought up among women, as you have been." Likewise, both Digory and Uncle Andrew are deeply impressed by Jadis ("Digory thought, 'She's wonderfully brave. And strong. She's what I call a Queen!'"). And of course, Digory, like Uncle Andrew, shows no regard for Polly's safety in order to do what he wants. In all of this, Lewis intends for us to recognize the great danger and temptation that lies before Digory (and perhaps before us as well).

(That we are to put ourselves in Digory's place becomes evident when we read Lewis, in one of his more didactic moments in the Chronicles, put the following warning in the mouth of Aslan in Chapter 15: "But you are growing more like [Charn]. It is not certain that some wicked one of your race will not find out a secret as evil as the Deplorable Word and use it to destroy all living things. And soon, very soon, before you are an old man and an old woman, great nations in your world will be ruled by tyrants who care no more for joy and justice and mercy than the Empress Jadis. Let your world beware.")

Living Within the Tao of Aslan

While Digory does succumb to the lust of curiosity in the Hall of Images, he eventually is able to resist the lust for power and make things right again. In seeing how he is able to stand, we ourselves can learn what it means to fight temptation like a true Narnian.

First, from the beginning Digory is able to see through Uncle Andrew's grand words about the high and lonely destiny. "All it means," he said to himself, "is that he thinks he can do anything he likes to get anything he wants" (Ch. 2). The first step in resisting temptation is the ability to recognize evil behind its many lofty disguises, and Digory displays the same wisdom expressed by Bunyan in *The Pilgrim's Progress* when he says, "It came burning hot into my mind, whatever he said and however he flattered, when he got me home to his house, he would sell me for a slave" (Lewis includes this quotation in the third chapter of *The Abolition of Man*).

Second, Digory lives within the *Tao*, within the ordered structure of the universe as God has made it. He is instinctively repulsed by Uncle Andrew's callousness toward animals and children, and conversely attracted to virtues like faithfulness, promise-keeping, compassion, and loyalty. The bond of friendship he shares with Polly helps to anchor him throughout the story.

Third, when confronted by Aslan, Digory refuses to whitewash his sin (though Aslan does prod him with a low growl), but instead forthrightly confesses his responsibility for bringing the Witch into Narnia. He does this knowing that his confession may ruin any hope of receiving a cure for his Mother's illness (Ch. 11).

Fourth, meeting Aslan solidifies his allegiance to the *Tao*, since the *Tao* is simply the expression of Aslan's will in the world. The Lion's kiss gives him new strength and courage, anchoring his resolve to obey and put right what he has broken. The breath of Aslan orders his affections, so that his love for his Mother is fitting and proper when he faces the Witch's diabolical temptation. He is able to resist because, in his encounter with Aslan, he has intuitively learned what Lewis expressed in a letter to Dom Bede Griffiths:

> Put first things first and we get second things thrown in: put second things first & we lose *both* first and second things. We never get, say, even the sensual pleasure of food at its best when we are being greedy.[56]

With Aslan's breath hanging upon him, Digory is rooted in the *Tao*, and thus prepared when Jadis offers life and health to his Mother at the expense of his integrity. Significantly, it is his relationship with Polly that is the light which exposes the Witch's lies.

And the meanness of the suggestion that he should leave Polly behind suddenly made all the other things the Witch had been saying to him sound false and hollow. (Ch. 13)

Reaping the Reward

So then, this is what it looks like to live in the *Tao* of Aslan: recognizing evil, confessing sin, cultivating friendships, refusing to use people, trusting the grace and compassion of the Lion, and putting first things first. And the fruit of such faithfulness is as generational as the Conditioner's lust for power. For by the grace of the Lion, Digory stands firm in the evil day, receiving the Lion's commendation and sowing the seed of the Tree that will protect Narnia for hundreds of years.

> "Son of Adam," said Aslan, "you have sown well. And you, Narnians, let it be your first care to guard this Tree, for it is your Shield. The Witch of whom I told you has fled far away into the North of the world; she will live on there, growing stronger in dark Magic. But while that Tree flourishes she will never come down into Narnia." (Ch. 14)

So also, we must sow well the Tree of Life, whose fruit is joy and peace and health, the aroma of life to some and death to others. Sowing is hard work, requiring hunger and thirst, blood and tears. But, in the Lord, we can be confident that our labor is never in vain (1 Cor. 15:58). We will reap, if we don't give up.

15

Tirian's Trials and Tragedy

Enduring Deep Doubt and the Soul's Dark Night

God does not shield his saints from Darkness. Many of us have drunk Terror, that uncontrolled passion that crashes in wave after seemingly endless wave upon the shores of a troubled mind. Personally, I have wept in the dark, trembling in the corner like a frightened child, unable to marshal thought or will to push back the fear. Others have no doubt known deeper darkness, longer nights. But I would not wish such loneliness, spiritual turmoil, and emotional panic on anyone, because I have tasted and seen that it has the flavor of hell.

In my life, I have had a number of seasons like this, what many call "dark nights of the soul." Some were caused directly by my sin, and the darkness was God's loving discipline to bring me to repentance. Others were only exacerbated by my sin, induced by causes I cannot fathom and then stirred up by the vestiges of rebellion that lurk in the black caves of the soul. I have met devils in the night, and watched helplessly as my supposed strength withered before them and left me terrified and alone. I have felt (however briefly) the tug of suicidal thoughts and the seductive promise of relief from the cares of the world.

For these reasons, *The Last Battle* has a peculiar kind of resonance for me. It is a story perched on the brink of despair, a story that then tumbles down the cliff into the abyss below. It is a tragic tale, filled with far more death than all of the other stories combined. Dryads are felled, Narnians are killed in Cair Paravel, Roonwit the Centaur lies dead with a Calormene arrow in his side, talking horses are shot by treacherous Dwarfs, the Boar and Bear fall in battle, as do some of the dogs. Even the heroes die in the end. The entire book is a sad journey to the grave (or rather, to the Stable Door).

Spiraling Down into Despair

But even more than the dominance of death, there is the constant tragedy, the inevitable march of bad news that shows the truthfulness of a side comment from *The Magician's Nephew*: "When things go wrong, you'll find they usually go on getting worse for some time" (Ch. 15). Every hope is dashed. Every bit of luck is followed by misfortune. Every moment of joy leads to calamity. Tirian rescues the Dwarfs, only to have them reject him and Aslan, demonstrating that Shift's lies have proven more devastating than he thought. Poggin the honest Dwarf defects and lifts the spirits of the faithful, but immediately Tash flies through the woods, sending shudders down their spines. They formulate a plan to retake Narnia and Jewel speaks of the long, peaceful, happy centuries of Narnian history, only to be interrupted by the grim news of Cair Paravel's conquest and Roonwit's death. During the battle with the Calormenes, the horses arrive as reinforcements, only to be shot down by the cynical Dwarfs. Until the end, you will look in vain for a moment of relief or happiness that is not quickly followed by calamity and evil. Every happy turn meets a dead end, and the story spirals down, down, down into despair.

But even more troubling than this descent into tragedy is the unsettling loss of theological ballast when it appears that Aslan has arrived, but horribly transformed. Lewis shields the reader from this disturbance, since we know that Shift has simply deceived the Narnians with a poorly disguised donkey. But for the characters, the disorientation is deep and profound, "as if the sun rose one day and were a black sun" (*The Last Battle*, Ch. 3). The truth is twisted, as all manner of wickedness and evil is justified in Aslan's name because, as everyone knows, "he's not a tame lion." Even Tirian and Jewel are initially deceived by this false theology as they each repeat it in an effort to understand the death of the Trees and the enslavement of the Narnians at Aslan's command.

That last phrase is key. In all the stories, Aslan has permitted and allowed (and even ordained and guided) evil actions and events. The White Witch's triumph, the Telmarine conquest of Narnia, Shasta's entire story—all of these were governed by the wise paw of Aslan for the ultimate good of his people. The situation in *The Last Battle* is very different. To Tirian, Aslan is not merely ordaining that evil exist; he is calling evil good. Aslan has come, but he is not Aslan. It is not unlike those dreams in which someone you love suddenly turns into something horrible right before your eyes.

Thus, the most disturbing challenge the heroes face is theological, which is why it resonates so deeply with me. My bleakest seasons of darkness and depression were triggered by theological questions and doubts. The vision of God and the world that I cherished so much began to come apart. I suppose it's a testimony to the centrality of Christ in my life that my soul came unglued when the doubts fell upon me, and I do take a kind of comfort in it (as I would encourage others to take should they find themselves in similar turmoil). It is not for nothing that the Bible says, "If the foundations are destroyed, what can the righteous do?" (Ps. 11:3). Nevertheless, the reality of Christ's centrality in my life was small consolation when my vision of him became cloudy, or twisted, or I begun to wonder whether he was there to be seen at all.

Tied to the Tree of Despair

It is bad enough to experience such doubts for a few days; it is worth when we are sent into the abyss of theological confusion for months at a time. The incessant questions, the nagging doubts, the paralyzing panic attacks, the false hopes followed by terrifying relapse, the constant fear that we are on the brink of falling beyond recovery, the fatalistic blanket that smothered all hope of ever escaping and leave our souls naked and numb—I can recall all of them, even if, on the far side of those valleys, I keep such thoughts at arm's length, lest they swell in strength and crash over me again. This is one of the peculiarities of all pain (or pleasure)—whether physical, emotional, or spiritual—and one that Lewis was well aware of.

> This is our dilemma—either to taste and not to know or to know and not to taste—or, more strictly, to lack one kind of knowledge because we are outside it. As thinkers we are cut off from what we think about; as tasting, touching, willing, living, hating, we do not clearly understand. The more lucidly we think, the more we are cut off: the more deeply we enter into reality, the less we can think. You cannot *study* Pleasure in the moment of the nuptial embrace, nor repentance while repenting, nor analyze the nature of humour while roaring with laughter. But when else can you really know these things? 'If only my toothache would stop, I could write another chapter about Pain.' But once it stops, what do I know about pain?[57]

But even at this distance, both in time and experience, the effects linger. Such dark nights leave their impression. They mark us, so that we walk with a limp all our days. I remember the desperate cries, the pleading prayers, the "O-God-where-are-you's" and "please-come-and-rescue-me's" and the "I-will-do-anything's." They still echo in the deep places of the soul, and I hear them in Tirian's desperation:

> And he called out "Aslan! Aslan! Aslan! Come and help us now."
> But the darkness and the cold and the quietness went on just the same. "Let me be killed," cried the King. "I ask nothing for myself. But come and save all Narnia." (Ch. 4)

Many saints have been tied to that tree. They have felt the blackness and despair, the unending silence and cold of night. How many of us have begged for "the Job moment," for Yahweh of hosts to appear in the whirlwind and kick down our door, even to thunder at us from the storm, ("Who do you think you are!?!"), for at least then we would know that he's real? For my own part, in all of my dark nights, the Job moment never came. Instead I have experienced (though not every time) something like what happens to the last king of Narnia.

> And still there was no change in the night or the wood, but there began to be a kind of change inside Tirian. Without knowing why, he began to feel a faint hope. And he felt somehow stronger. (Ch. 4)

Embracing Dark Adventures Together

So then, *The Last Battle* shows us tragedy and despair. Does it also show us how to endure? Can it instruct Narnians how to live in the dark and "take the adventure that Aslan sends to us"? I believe that it can.

One of the more obvious reasons that Tirian and the faithful Narnians persevere under trials is the fact that they face them together. The friendship of Tirian and Jewel keeps them grounded when everything else in their world gives way. Their love and affection for one another is deep and manifest, and pre-dates any of their troubles. The lesson is that we must prepare for dark nights by cultivating strong relationships while it is yet light. "A friend loves at all times, and a brother is born for adversity" (Prov. 17:17).

> Two are better than one, because they have a good reward for their toil. For if they fall, one will lift up his fellow. But woe to him who is alone when he falls and has not another to lift him up! Again, if two lie together, they keep warm, but how can one keep warm alone? And though a man might prevail against one who is alone, two will withstand him—a threefold cord is not quickly broken. (Eccles. 4:9–12)

Fightings Without and Fears Within

A second way to prepare to stand firm in the evil day is to know your enemies, both those without and those within. Other chapters have shown how various villains in the Chronicles embody the rebellious worldly apostles that beckon us today. In *The Last Battle* Shift is the old and ugly face of false and manipulative friendships. Ginger the Cat and Rishda Tarkaan express the shrewdness of "enlightened" atheism that hides behind a veneer of religious language. Thus, we must learn to identify the Ancient Serpent's song in our own world.

More importantly, we must come to understand the enemy within. External enemies are no true threat unless their lies find a willing embrace in our hearts and minds. We must not be malleable and simplistic like Puzzle, lest we fall prey to sneaky apes. For myself, I have learned that the voice in my head that never gives me rest, the one that badgers me with incessant questions, the one that endlessly stokes the flames of doubt—that voice is not my friend. When I encounter him, I must remember that the goal is not to best him in a debate, but to put him to death (Col. 3:5).

Along these lines, my own struggles have taught me the importance of doubting my doubts. In the pit, doubt can feel so certain, so unassailable, so indubitable, which is an odd thing when you come to think of it. Why is it only the Truth that must defend itself? Why is Unbelief asking all of the accusatory questions? Who died and made him king? Why doesn't Doubt have to take his seat in the dock and give an account? (Incidentally, I'm not suggesting that you get in a debate with your doubts. While there is certainly a place for wrestling through honest questions with trustworthy friends and counselors, most of the time it's wise to avoid the endless back-and-forth in your head. As the Narnians learned in *The Silver Chair,* it is no use arguing with the devil on his (or her) terms; far better to pick up a sword and kill the dragon.)

God-Forsaken and Still Obedient

Third, root yourself in true knowledge of and obedience to the Great Lion. Tirian knows the truth, and it steels him against deception when he's tied to the tree and sees a lion-like shape come out of the stable.

> He had never seen the Great Lion. He had never seen a common lion. He couldn't be sure that what he saw was not the real Aslan. He had not expected Aslan to look like that stiff thing which stood and said nothing. But how could one be sure? For a moment horrible thoughts went through his mind: then he remembered the nonsense about Tash and Aslan being the same and knew that the whole thing must be a cheat. (Ch. 4)

Tirian has the Truth in his bones, and it guards him from the horrible thoughts which run through his mind.

In the midst of doubt and depression, a large part of obedience means avoiding idleness at all costs. Though all of his plans come to naught, Tirian is never without one. He never gives into despair, but continues to hope, continues to seek help, continues to obey, even in the darkest moments. Likewise, we must never use our doubts as an excuse for further sin; that will only make things worse. George MacDonald was right to say, "Obedience is the great opener of eyes." And obedience may be as small as getting up and sweeping the floor (rather than sulking in bed). Manual labor never abolished my doubts, but by the grace of God it did help to make them bearable.

Lewis stresses the centrality of obedience when we feel lost and abandoned in a quotation from *The Screwtape Letters* that I mentioned in an earlier chapter (as Paul might say: to quote the same things is no trouble for me, and it is safe for you):

> Our cause is never more in danger than when a human, no longer desiring, but still intending, to do our Enemy's will, looks round upon a universe from which every trace of Him seems to have vanished, and asks why he has been forsaken, and still obeys.[58]

Obedience also includes resisting with all of our might the false fatalism that threatens to suffocate our faith. In his dark moments, Tirian may have doubted Aslan, but doubt and faith can exist side by side ("I do believe; help my unbelief," Mark 9:24). What Tirian never does is give into hopelessness. He continues to believe that Aslan is able to break in, that he can and will send help, that however things may look, he will never leave us nor forsake us.

Filling Our Nostrils with Narnian Air

Finally, I should mention that in addition to rooting myself in the true knowledge of God, and in addition to seeking to trust and obey God in the dark, and in addition to surrounding myself with gospel-breathing, praying people who loved me, one of the primary means that God has used to sustain my faith in the darkest times is the Narnian stories themselves. They inevitably draw me out of the prison of my own mind and put me in touch with something True, something Good, something Beautiful, something Solid and Stable and Secure when all around my soul gives way.

Breathing Narnian air has strengthened me in the pit, kept me believing when my faith went wobbly. The stories have delivered me from the Dwarfish cynicism that is worse than death, the enslaving inability to believe the obvious because, being so afraid of being taken in, I refuse to be taken out. They have given me courage in the blackest night because I have known in my bones that I am now, as always, between the paws of the true Aslan.

16

The Glory of a Narnian Queen

Standing in Awe of the Peculiar Majesty of Women

C. S. Lewis lived most of his life as a bachelor, and all of the Chronicles were written during his unmarried days. However, toward the end of his life, he developed a friendship and then a romance with Joy Davidman, an American poet and writer. They were wed in 1956, but their marital bliss was tragically cut short by cancer, and Joy died in 1960. Lewis wrote that "for those few years [Joy] and I feasted on love; every mode of it: solemn and merry, romantic and realistic, sometimes as dramatic as a thunderstorm, sometimes as comfortable and unemphatic as putting on your soft slippers. No cranny of heart or body remained unsatisfied."[59] Given the intensity of their love, it's no surprise to find Lewis write the following about the awe-inspiring wonder of a good wife:

> A good wife contains so many persons in herself. What was [Joy] not to me? She was my daughter and my mother, my pupil and my teacher, my subject and my sovereign, and always holding all these in solution, my

trusty comrade, friend, shipmate, fellow soldier. My mistress, but at the same time all that any man friend (and I have good ones) has ever been to me. . . . Solomon calls his bride Sister. Could a woman be a complete wife unless, for a moment, in one particular mood, a man felt almost inclined to call her Brother?[60]

Some regard Lewis's sentiment here as evidence for a movement at the end of his life toward sexual egalitarianism, and therefore a deviation from his earlier, more "complementarian" view of masculinity and femininity. I agree with those others who find this poetic and romantic expression to be in full concord with Lewis's lifelong embrace of the ordered beauty of gender complementarity. Indeed, for me it confirms that his marriage to Joy Davidman brought on a deepening awe and wonder at the glorious "other" called woman.

Watching in Wonder from the Outside

Before venturing into Narnia, a brief explanation for why this chapter finds itself at the end of this book, and why, unlike other chapters, it will be a thematic survey of all seven books in the Chronicles, rather than a focused exploration of one or two. In other words, I devoted entire chapters to Edmund's transformation, to Peter's knighthood, to Lune's kingship, to Shasta and Digory— why write one cumulative chapter on the female characters?

The first thing to be said is that it has nothing whatever do with any kind of misogynistic nonsense about the importance of women, either in Narnia or in our world. As the son of a mother, the husband of a wife, and the friend of numerous women, I agree entirely with Lewis that women (or at least particular women) are frequently men's equals (if that's the right word) and often betters when it comes to piety, zeal, learning, and charity.[61] Nor is the compression of Narnian femininity into one chapter because I think women are less likely to be interested in Narnia. When I have taught classes or participated in discussions on the Chronicles, women are as likely (if not more likely) to be enthusiastic, engaged, and insightful readers of the books.

No, the reason is quite simple: when it comes to the female characters, I am an outsider. All of these chapters are written from where I sit, and their subject-matter has been determined by the things that move me the most. For me, to live like a Narnian means to aspire to be a Knight of the Order of the Lion or a King of Archenland. I have a deep appreciation and admiration for the female characters, and insofar as we are talking about those Narnian (and Christian) virtues that are mutually shared and expressed, I have learned as much from Lucy and Polly as I have from Peter and Lune.

But when it comes to the feminine virtues—not just royal grandeur, but the peculiar majesty of a *Queen*—I watch in wonder from the outside. The bright glory of womanhood is almost ineffable, and in its presence I find myself feeling a bit shy, like Adam must have felt when he woke up and saw Eve for the first time. I feel the deep commonality, the mutual humanity, the this-at-last-ness and bone-of-my-bone-ness that comes from the shared image we bear. And yet there is the inescapable otherness, the irreducible foreignness of a Rib Re-Made and Re-Fashioned. Like me, but different. Same, but sundered. Such is the splendor of the fairer sex, the one whom Paul calls "The Glory of Man."

The Struggle to Show the Glory of Femininity

Lewis himself felt this awe at feminine strength and grace, and I believe struggled at times to convey its distinctive characteristics in the Narnia stories. To take one example, the feminine appreciation for aesthetics, particularly when it comes to dress and clothing, is something that he recognizes as worthy of admiration, but also something he knows can become silly and foolish. But how to depict both sides in the stories? He portrays the latter through the Tarkeena Lasaraleen, who is preoccupied with "clothes and parties and gossip," prattling on about her dress and other trivialities despite the obvious agitation and earnestness of Aravis (*The Horse and His Boy*, Ch. 7).

On the other hand, Lewis doesn't want to give the impression that a proper concern for dresses and appearances and so forth is somehow inherently silly or wrong. Thus, when Aravis arrives at Anvard and meets Lucy, we read,

> "You'd like to come and see them, wouldn't you?" said Lucy, kissing Aravis. They liked each other at once and soon went away together to talk about Aravis's bedroom and Aravis's boudoir and about getting clothes for her, and all the sort of things girls do talk about on such an occasion. (Ch. 15)

There is no trace of condescension here, for Lucy (as we'll see) is the most spiritually attuned of the Pevensies, and can arguably be regarded as Lewis's favorite. In my judgment, Lewis is attempting to recover a kind of girlish innocence in Aravis, who to this point has been dismissive of such things, preferring "bows and arrows and horses and dogs and swimming" to "palaces and pearls." Lewis, I think, doesn't want to give the impression that girls are only admirable if they have the same interests as the typical boy. A similar scene appears in *The Magician's Nephew*, where Polly leads the way into the Hall of Images because she is more interested than Digory in the magnificent clothes of the royal figures.

Of course, the response might be that Lewis shows his preference for masculine concerns over feminine in the fact that Susan is "no longer a friend of Narnia" because she is "interested in nothing nowadays except nylons and lipsticks and invitations." However, Susan is not rejected because of her feminine interests, but because of a particular kind of silliness and immaturity. As Polly says, "I wish she would grow up. She wasted all her school time wanting to be the age she is now, and she'll waste all the rest of her life trying to stay that age. Her whole idea is to race on to the silliest time of one's life as quick as she can and then stop there as long as she can" (*The Last Battle*, Ch. 12).

Lewis expressed a similar disdain for those adults who are overly concerned with being grown up.

> To be concerned about being grown up, to admire the grown up because it is grown up, to blush at the suspicion of being childish; these things are the marks of childhood and adolescence. And in childhood and adolescence they are, in moderation, healthy symptoms. Young things ought to want to grow. But to carry on into middle life or even into early manhood this concern about being adult is a mark of really arrested development.[62]

Thus, Lewis struggles, as only a man can do, to understand and communicate a basic feature of feminine glory, and its perverse and foolish imitation. The popularity of his books among women and girls testifies to some measure of his success.

The Intuition of Narnian Queens

We turn now to consider some of the qualities that Lewis seems to particularly associate with his heroines. The first and most prominent feature is the role of the female characters as the intuition or guiding lights of the stories. We begin, naturally enough, with Lewis's favorite, Lucy Pevensie. Of all the Narnian characters, Lucy is the most attuned to the will of Aslan. As Edmund says, "Lucy sees him most often" (*The Voyage of the Dawn Treader*, Ch. 7), and the narrator at one point comments that Lucy "understood some of his moods."

The night Aslan dies, Lucy is the first to mention her horrible feeling, "as if something were hanging over us. . . . Something about Aslan. Either some dreadful thing is going to happen to him, or something dreadful that he's going to do" (*The Lion, the Witch, and the Wardrobe*, Ch. 14). It is she and Susan that comfort Aslan on his sad and lonely walk to the Stone Table. Likewise, the two girls are the first witnesses of his resurrection, echoing the Gospel accounts of Mary Magdalene and the other women, and as a result they enjoy a marvelous chase with the risen Lion.

> Round and round the hilltop he led them, now hopelessly out of their reach, now letting them almost catch his tail, now diving between them, now tossing them in the air with his huge and beautifully velveted paws and catching them again, and now stopping unexpectedly so that all three of them rolled over together in a happy laughing heap of fur and arms and legs. It was such a romp as no one has ever had except in Narnia; and whether it was more like playing with a thunderstorm or playing with a kitten Lucy could never make up her mind. (Ch. 15)

In *Prince Caspian*, it is Lucy who first sees Aslan and understands his desire for them to follow, even without being told. It is Lucy that Aslan wakens in the night, calling her to himself, and giving her the hard task of guiding the others across the gorge. The Lion is at first visible only to her, until the others, through listening to her wisdom, come to see him (*Prince Caspian*, Ch. 10–11). Further examples of Lucy's close relationship with Aslan could be multiplied, and many of the most memorable lines in the stories occur in conversations between her and the Lion.

But Lucy is not the only female character who is blessed with deep, spiritual and practical intuition. Hwin the horse is described as "a very sensible mare," and is favorably contrasted with Bree in his pride and conceit. In the search for Prince Rilian, it is Jill who is entrusted with remembering the signs, repeating them to herself every morning and night. Later, in *The Last Battle*, King Tirian appoints her to guide the faithful in the dark, recognizing her obvious skill in following the stars. When Digory and Polly arrive in Charn, Polly is the one who immediately senses that something is wrong with the place, and rightly urges them to leave. In fact, Polly's intuition is regularly on display throughout that story, and Digory's life would have been far easier had he listened to her. The Chronicles do contain flippant dismissals of the counsel and advice of women, but significantly, such condescending remarks are placed in the mouth of Uncle Andrew, who dismisses Digory because he's been raised by women, and Digory himself, in his most Andrew-like moments. The picture that emerges is one in which the male characters are the overall leaders, but the female characters are the wise counselors and guides, whose intuition is not to be ignored. The lesson for Christian marriages, families, and churches is plain.

The Graceful Beauty of Glad-Hearted Submission

Beyond their intuition, the Narnian ladies display other admirable feminine qualities. Lucy is a healer, using her cordial to mend wounds and restore health to many. Queen Susan the Gentle is known for her graciousness and beauty, and in *The Horse and His Boy*, she displays a mother's concern and protectiveness for Shasta (whom she believes to be Prince Corin). The description of the Cabby's wife Nellie (later Queen Helen) highlights her domesticity, her manners, and her shyness. Both Lucy and Polly show the simplicity of mercy when they promptly forgive and make peace with Peter and Digory, respectively. All of the Narnian queens are praised for their beauty, grace, tenderness, and compassion.

Additionally, the heroines possess a deep sense of the beauty and propriety of submission to godly authority. When Edmund begins to quarrel with Peter in *Prince Caspian*, Lucy whispers to him, "Hadn't we better do what Peter says? He is the High King, you know." At the same time, Lucy is willing to disobey Peter later in the story, when she has been given clear instructions from Aslan to follow whether the others do or not. Lucy knows that ultimately she must obey Aslan, not man (High King or otherwise), but that obedience to Aslan often includes deference, honor, and submission to those whom he appoints over us.

In *The Silver Chair*, Jill implies that such submission extends to the marital relationship. The enchanted Prince is prattling on about his coming reign in Overland and how he will do all by the Emerald Lady's counsel and her word shall be his law. Jill, expressing an affinity for the headship of a husband, says, "Where I come from, they don't think much of men who are bossed about by their wives." The Prince responds in a patronizing manner, saying, "Shalt think otherwise when thou hast a man of thine own, I warrant you" (*The Silver Chair*, Ch. 11). The conversation finds a precedent in Lewis's words on the subject in *Mere Christianity*.

> Even a woman who wants to be the head of her own house does not usually admire the same state of things when she finds it going on next door. She is much more likely to say 'Poor Mr X! Why he allows that appalling woman to boss him about the way she does is more than I can imagine.' I do not think she is even very flattered if anyone mentions the fact of her own 'headship'. There must be something unnatural about the rule of wives over husbands, because the wives themselves are half ashamed of it and despise the husbands whom they rule.[63]

The Bright Bravery of a Lioness

Finally, a chapter on the ladies of Narnia would not be complete without some description of their strength, bravery, and loyalty. Aravis is described as "true as steel" and would never dream of deserting a companion, whether she liked him or not (*The Horse and His Boy*, Ch. 6). Lucy's courage wins the admiration of Caspian and the rest, when she volunteers to venture into the magician's house on behalf of the Monopods (*The Voyage of the Dawn Treader*, Ch. 9). Polly shows herself to be a true and faithful friend to Digory, when she asks to travel with him on his errand to the west (*The Magician's Nephew*, Ch. 12).

And of course, at times the ladies prove their valor in battle, with both Jill and Lucy performing capable feats of archery when the need arises (Prince Corin says that in battle, Lucy is "as good as a man, or at any rate as good as a boy..." *The Horse and His Boy*, Ch. 13). Some have detected a contradiction, or perhaps a shift in Lewis's view on the propriety of women in combat. In *The Lion, the Witch, and the Wardrobe*, Father Christmas tells Susan and Lucy that he does not intend for them to engage in the coming battle, for "battles are ugly when women fight." Nevertheless, he gives them both weapons and tells them to use them "only in great need" (Ch. 10). In truth, there is no tension between these directions and the later practice. The point is simply this: if given the choice, women ought not fight in battle. However, in emergencies (such as when an army makes a surprise attack on an ally, or when there are only a handful of faithful Narnians fighting dozens of Calormenes and traitors), women too can show themselves valiant in war.

Much more could be said about the heroines of Narnia. Their intuition, their beauty, their grace, their compassion and loyalty and courage are worthy of the highest praise and esteem. To imitate them, to join them in the happy laughter of a Narnian romp, is to become a true Queen of Narnia: "bright and brave, full of gloriously feminine, passionate, and often strongly insistent energy."[64] Solomon celebrates her when he says, "Who is she that looks forth like the dawn, fair as the moon, clear as the sun, and terrible as an army with banners?" (Song 6:10). Such a lady is a vibrant and potent force for good in the world, showing by her glad-hearted tenderness and lion-strength that she too has buried her face in Aslan's mane and become a lioness.

Epilogue

More Narnian Hills to Explore

As I read again through the Chronicles in writing this book, I was repeatedly struck with how many chapters could have been written. There were dozens of places where I would have loved to stop and pitch my tent for a time, unpacking Lewis's subtlety and suggestiveness. But just like the Shadow-lands, all books must end. But as this one does, I would like to point the reader in some directions to run, places where this book might have gone, but didn't. Some of these are relatively minor sites, worth mentioning but perhaps not dwelling upon. Others are substantial peaks, worthy of book-length treatments. And even these don't exhaust all that there is to see. So without further ado, here are some Narnian hills worth exploring:

- Polly is a true and thoughtful friend, the rare kind that love you enough to tell you how wrong you are, and stand by you even when you're being a silly idiot. I want to be (and have) that kind of friend.
- Shift is a terrible friend, who ought to be eaten by a gigantic bird-monster. Too many of us know how to manipulate others just like that ugly ape.

- I think that Lewis intends for us to see ourselves in the Dufflepuds. And that ought to make us stop and think.
- Twice in the books (once in *Prince Caspian* and once in *The Magician's Nephew*) one of the characters says something like, "A son of Adam has arisen to rule and name the animals." Now this is an obvious allusion to the creation story in Genesis 1–2, but the connection that Lewis is making between kingship and naming, between man's dominion and man's capacity to speak and label, is worth spending a lot of time reflecting upon. Someone should write a book about it.
- Aslan gets bigger as we get older. Discuss.
- *Prince Caspian* is a book about the incredible worth and value of Old Things and Ancient Stories. Two thousand years after the resurrection of Jesus, that's something worth remembering.
- Eustace appears as a major character in three books, and his transformation is both fascinating and profound. By the end, he no longer deserves his name, but he's also the sort of boy who wouldn't mind that he had it.
- Lewis portrays the absolute necessity of spiritual disciplines in *The Silver Chair* ("Remember the signs. Nothing else matters"). We live down here in the fog where it's hard to think. The signs elevate us to Aslan's country where we know what we're here for. They guide us and lead us when we meditate upon them day and night. And, of course, when we muff them, Aslan gives grace and still guides us. As Puddleglum says, "There are no accidents."
- The Narnian creation narrative is glorious, with echoes of Genesis, the Psalms, Job, the Middle Ages, and Tolkien. This world is God's song, and his music resounds in every place. Which is to say, you should read Michael Ward's books on Narnia.
- I almost wrote a chapter on True Narnia called "Further Up and Further In." Then I realized that it would just be a string of quotations from *The Last Battle* intermixed with others from *The Great Divorce* and *The Weight of Glory*. I am profoundly unqualified to write such a chapter, so I'll just point you to those works

by Lewis, and encourage you to meditate on the fact that the further in you go, the bigger and closer everything gets.

And with that, I'd like to thank you for taking the time to read this little book. It was my great privilege to host you. If you should ever find yourself in Archenland, stop in and see King Lune. He's a friend of mine (more like a relative really), and if you mention my name, he'll almost surely pull out the aged wine and set forth a feast you'll not soon forget.

Appendix

A Short Q&A with the Author

The following interview with the author was conducted by the Faun Tumnus, who was granted a special dispensation to phone the author at home. It has been lightly edited for clarity. Headings have been added for easy reference.

FT: Professor Rigney, thank you for taking the time to talk with me this morning.

JR: My pleasure.

The Proper Ordering of the Books

FT: I wanted to take a few moments to ask you some questions that often come up about the Narnia books. First, what do you think is the proper ordering of the books?

JR: The original one—the one based on order of publication:
The Lion, the Witch, and the Wardrobe
Prince Caspian
The Voyage of the Dawn Treader
The Silver Chair

>   *The Horse and His Boy*
>   *The Magician's Nephew*
>   *The Last Battle*
>   That's the order I followed in the composition of this present
>   volume.

FT: That's interesting. The current publishers often put it in
chronological order beginning with *The Magician's Nephew*
because they say that's what C. S. Lewis wanted.

JR: Yes, they say that, but you can't always believe everything an
author tells you.

FT: Who said so?

JR: Lewis did actually—in a short essay called "It All Began with
a Picture." But everyone knows it; ask anybody you like.

FT: You're sounding a bit like Edmund after he ate the Turkish
Delight.

JR: Actually, it's the publishers who are on the side of the White
Witch. Look, there are a number of reasons that might be
given for putting *The Lion, The Witch, and the Wardrobe* first,
but I'll just give you the main one that ought to settle the matter. In the book, when Mr. Beaver says to the children "Aslan
is on the move," we are treated to this wonderful passage
about the effect of Aslan's name on them. In the midst of that,
the narrator says, "None of the children knew who Aslan was
any more than you do." This tells me that Lewis was aiming
for a very particular effect in this scene, building anticipa-
tion for the moment when we'll finally meet Aslan. Likewise,
when Aslan comes up again later, the children are excited
(as the reader is meant to be), and then Lucy asks if Aslan is
a man, and we get the bit about Aslan being a Lion and the
King of the Wood and the Son of the Emperor-beyond-the-
Sea, and that he's not safe, but good.

The point is: all of this build-up to meeting Aslan is ruined
on the first time through if you've followed the publishers and
read *The Magician's Nephew* first, since you'd know exactly

who Aslan was.

FT: Why then did Lewis say that the books could be introduced in chronological order?

JR: I'd like to ask him myself. I suspect because he'd forgotten some of those little details, which I think he intended to be highly influential in creating a particular effect on his readers. I'd like to think that if someone pointed out what I just said, he'd retract the nonsense about the chronological order. Of course, the question of order mainly comes up for first-time readers. I'd strongly suggest reading them in the traditional order. After you've read through them in that order, then go back and read whichever ones you like.

What to Make of Emeth, the Calormene Soldier

FT: A question about some of the theology in the books. Many Christians wonder what they should do with Emeth, the Calormene soldier who reaches Aslan's country in *The Last Battle*. What do you make of him?

JR: So you've heard of Christians, have you? And you're keeping up with our theological debates? Not bad for a Faun. I've heard Doug Wilson make a number of great points about Emeth's place in the stories. First, we need to recognize that while Narnia is a "supposal" (see the Introduction) with strong Christian themes, there's not a one-to-one correspondence between Narnia and our world. For example, there is no Narnian Great Commission, a command from Aslan to go into all the world and make disciples of all the nations. In this sense, the world of Narnia is much more like the world of the Old Testament than the New Testament. You have Aslan and his people in Narnia, other nations which are distinct from Narnia but still are allied with Aslan (like Archenland and the Islands), and then nations that worship other gods (like Calormen). This is very similar to Israel, nations like Tyre who at various times in their history worship Yahweh (Hiram of Tyre helps David and Solomon build the temple), and then the other nations that worship other false gods (like Moab, Syria, and Babylon). And of course, in the Old Testament, Gentiles could worship Yahweh without becoming Jews (think of Melchizedek, who is a priest of the Most High God, and Job, who may be an Edomite king). In that sense, Emeth might be someone like the Queen of Sheba, who eventually travels to Israel under Solomon and is so moved by God's blessing that she says, "Blessed be Yahweh your God, who has delighted in you."

All of this is to say, Lewis may not be as off base as it seems on first glance. Of course, the problem is that Emeth is a sincere Tash worshiper and Aslan accepts for himself all the good service done in the name of Tash, and Tash accepts all vile service done in the name of Aslan. This makes it sound as though a sincere Baal worshiper who keeps his oath and shows himself honorable would be embraced by Yahweh. That, it seems to me, would be very problematic from a biblical point of view. After all, Yahweh is committed to his name being *known* among the nations.

But even here, we should recognize that Emeth's name is the Hebrew word for "truth," and Emeth's character and actions are strange if he is taking his cues from Tash. Tash is a bloodthirsty, cruel, and vile deity who accepts human sacrifice. Emeth is noble, truthful, and courageous. This is an odd case where the worshiper is *not* becoming like what he worships.

In the end, while I think my comments mitigate some of the problems with Emeth, I still don't think Lewis got this one quite right. I agree with Wilson that we should consider this, not a strikeout, but at the very least a foul ball.

FT: Why do you think Lewis would include something like this in his books?

JR: I think it's likely that Lewis believed something very much like it. It may be that this is his attempt to create a category for admitting into heaven noble pagans that he loved, like Plato, Aristotle, and so forth. There's a long tradition in the church of theologians attempting to find a way to get philosophers like that into heaven. Or it could just be that Lewis doesn't want his readers to get the impression that Calormenes are all bad and evil, that it was possible for them to come to know Aslan in some real way. And lastly, I think Lewis is trying to show that, as Aslan says to Emeth, "all find what they truly seek." The fact that Emeth had been seeking Something so long and so truly indicates that, perhaps, he was only responding to Aslan's call. As Aslan says to Jill on another occasion, no one calls upon him unless he first calls to them.

Loving Aslan Too Much?

FT: Another theological question. Some readers are so moved by the beauty of Aslan, that they begin to worry that they love the Lion of Narnia more than Jesus. What would you say to such people?

JR: That's a great question. In fact, Lewis himself was asked that once, when a mother wrote to him about her son Laurence who was worried that he loved Aslan more than Jesus. He responded, "Laurence can't *really* love Aslan more than Jesus, even if he feels that's what he is doing. For the things he loves Aslan for doing or saying are simply the things Jesus really did and said. So that when Laurence thinks he is loving Aslan, he is really loving Jesus: and perhaps loving Him more than he ever did before."[65]

This fits perfectly with what Lewis said about "sneaking past the watchful dragons." His whole goal in Narnia is to enable the gospel of Jesus to appear in its true potency, so that when you're loving Aslan, you're truly loving Jesus. If for some reason you find yourself deeply moved by Aslan, but have trouble transferring that to Jesus, then I would pray that God would give you a better imagination so that you're able to make the leap from Aslan to Jesus. After all, Lewis means for us to see Aslan as Jesus. "There [that is, in our world] I have another name. You must learn to know me by that name" (*The Voyage of the Dawn Treader*, Ch. 16). What I find encouraging in this passage is that Lewis expects us to make the connection between Aslan and Jesus, and that this connection doesn't always automatically happen. It's something that we must "learn." Hopefully, this book can be an aid in that learning process.

Introducing the Books to Children

FT: Very helpful, thank you. Back to the issue of introducing the books to children. What's the right way to do that?

JR: I don't think there's a single right way to introduce children to Narnia, just as there isn't one right way to introduce your children to Jesus and the gospel. After all, none of the children in the stories get into Narnia in exactly the same way: Lucy stumbles in out of curiosity, the others fall in while hiding, Eustace tumbles in through a picture frame, Jill gets in by asking, and Polly and Digory use the rings and pools. None of them are "better" or more "right." And as Aslan tells Lucy, "things never happen the same way twice."

I would say that it is important that parents live like Narnians first; that's one reason I've written this book. You want your children to recognize their home in the life and joy and nobility of Narnia. Beyond that, it's up to you.

Should We Tell Children the Deeper Meaning?

FT: You have young boys. How do you plan to introduce them? Will you tell them all about the Christian symbolism that's behind it?

JR: Yes, I thought I'd lead with that bit about Freud and Feuerbach; I think my four-year-old would love it.

In truth, my plan is to read them the stories simply as stories, and resist the urge to unpack all of the layers, particularly the explicitly Christian ones. Personally, one of the great joys of my life is the pleasure of discovery, of insight, of seeing something with my own eyes and "on my own" (though in reality, we always see with help). I'd like to give that gift of discovery to my boys. My hope is that one day they come up to me and say something like, "Dad, is Aslan Jesus?" I'd just smile and say, "Why do you say that?"

At the same time, I have no doubt that I'll appeal to certain qualities and characteristics in the books in order to help them navigate their own young lives: the necessity of hard obedience, the need to repent and confess sins sincerely, and so forth. And I certainly don't think there's anything wrong with parents telling their kids about the Christian side of things right from the get-go. Again, there's no universal right way.

Narnia on the Big Screen

FT: Staying with the theme of introducing people to Narnia, what do you think of the recent movie adaptations?

JR: (with a low growl) Don't get me started.

FT: I take it you're not a fan?

JR: That's putting it mildly. Look, in themselves, they're typical Hollywood movies that are safe for the whole family. And if that's all they were, I'd be content. But as adaptations of Narnia, I think they fail in some significant ways. And not silly things, like the additions of characters and scenes which aren't in the books at all. All of that is perfectly understandable when adapting a book to film, and when done well, is just fine. My problem is that I think the writers and producers have poisoned the air of Narnia. They're pumping a whole lot of 21st century American gas into the place, and it's getting so smoggy that everything is unrecognizable and some of the Dryads are withering.

FT: Care to elaborate a bit?

JR: Well, it's somewhat difficult to describe, but it has to do with the "feel" of the movie. Lewis comments on this sort of thing in his essay "On Stories." In fact, in that essay he discusses the film adaptation of *King Solomon's Mines*, a book that Lewis read and enjoyed as a child. The entire movie was ruined for him because, when it came to the final danger faced by the heroes, the filmmaker substituted a volcanic eruption and earthquake for the book's grim prospect of starving to death in the cave. The former was more exciting and cinematic, but, Lewis says, you lose "the whole sense of the deathly—the cold, the silence, and the surrounding faces of the ancient, the crowned and sceptred, dead." His point is that there is a great difference between "the hushing spell" of being trapped underground and "the rapid flutter of nerves" when the volcano erupts. It's that sort of qualitative difference that I have in mind.

FT: Interesting. Can you flesh this out a bit more?

JR: Think for a moment about the characters. In most movie adaptations, the names are changed to protect the innocent. In Narnia, the guilty change the characters, but leave the names intact. Peter, Susan, Edmund, and Lucy are all present and accounted for, but the quality of their characters is distorted from the books. Some of them are almost unrecognizable.

Incidentally, the best treatment of the movies can be found in an article in *Touchstone* magazine by Steven Boyer entitled "Narnia Invaded." You can find it online, as well as a follow-up lecture that he did on *The Voyage of the Dawn Treader* called "Hierarchy, Holiness, and Hollywood," which can be seen on YouTube.

FT: Since I'm not sure how to get on this "line" you speak of, and I've never even heard of Mount Yute Oob, could you unpack Boyer's argument a bit?

JR: I suppose that would be alright, though I would encourage everyone to find the article and read it. The full title is "Narnia Invaded: How the New Films Subvert Lewis's Hierarchical World." Boyer rightly argues that Lewis was fond of hierarchy and ordered relationships. His favorite analogy for hierarchy was "the Dance," and he recognized it in human relationships, in the cosmic order, and even in God. Regarding the latter he writes,

> In Christianity God is not a static thing—not even a person—but a dynamic, pulsating activity, a life, almost a kind of drama. Almost, if you will not think me irreverent, a kind of dance. The union between the Father and the Son is such a live concrete thing that this union itself is also a Person.[66]

He depicts the beauty of the Cosmic Dance in one of the final scenes in *Perelandra*. And in *The Voyage of the Dawn Treader*, Coriakin says that at some point, he will rise again in the east and tread the great dance. And, of course, this Trinitarian and cosmic order and beauty and structure ought to be imaged forth in human relationships:

> And now, what does it all matter? It matters more than anything else in the world. The whole dance, or drama, or pattern of this three-Personal life is to be played out in each one of us: or (put-

ting it the other way round) each one of us has got to enter that pattern, take his place in that dance. There is no other way to the happiness for which we were made. [67]

And in another place, Lewis is even more explicit:

I do not believe God created an egalitarian world. I believe the authority of the parent over the child, the husband over the wife, the learned over the simple, to have been as much a part of the original plan as the authority of man over beast. [68]

Of course, Lewis also affirmed the necessity of certain types of equality, but he embraced them as medicine, as protection against the inevitable abuse of hierarchy brought on by our sin. Nevertheless he thought it absolutely essential that we continue to embrace the inherent goodness of ordered and hierarchical relationships; failure to do so is a kind of disease:

The man who cannot conceive a joyful and loyal obedience on the one hand, nor an unembarrassed and noble acceptance of that obedience on the other, the man who has never even wanted to kneel or to bow, is a prosaic barbarian. [69]

If you want to follow-up on Lewis's vision of hierarchy, read his essays: "Membership," "Equality," and "Priestesses in the Church?" Or just read Narnia and *The Space Trilogy*.

FT: So how do the films get this wrong?

JR: In a variety of ways, but I'll just mention a few (though you can see Boyer's article for a much more detailed analysis). The primary way is the constant bickering and fighting between Caspian and Peter in the second film. They fight when they meet, they can't agree about plans, and when their plan ultimately fails, they blame and insult each other almost to the point of blows. There is not even a hint of this in the books. I agree with Boyer, that in the fundamental changes to the main characters, the filmmakers are evidently disciples of Miraz the Usurper, who can't fathom the reign of the two kings and two queens of Narnia because, as he says, "How could there be two kings at the same time?" How indeed, if they are both squabbling and quarrelling babies like Caspian and Peter!

Other instances could be mentioned: the message of the first film is that true maturity comes when we learn to *disobey* (something Lewis would find appalling), the transformation of Susan into a warrior princess (dropping Father Christmas's line about the ugliness of women in combat), the mutation of Caspian into a moody and revenge-seeking punk. But the really grievous nature of the movies comes from the opening scene of *Prince Caspian*, where Peter has just gotten into a fight (not for the first time) because he's tired of being treated like a kid and believes himself to be entitled to absolute deference from others. The director explains his motivation thusly:

> I always felt. . . . how hard it must have been, particularly for Peter, to have gone from being high king to going back to high school, and what that would do to him, do to his ego. . . . I always thought that would be a really hard thing for a kid to go through.

This sentiment makes me want to pull out my hair. It just shows how little the filmmakers understand Lewis's larger theological vision. They have no concept of the effect of breathing Narnian air on the children (and the readers and viewers). I can't say it better than Boyer:

> In Lewis's telling of all of the *Narnia* tales, the children's experiences as kings and queens in Narnia consistently transform them into nobler, more virtuous people in their own world. They are not spoiled children wanting to be kings again; they are noble

kings who carry that very nobility back into their non-royal roles as schoolchildren.

That's absolutely right, and I've tried to communicate some of that in this book through the noble knights, good-hearted kings, and faithful and obedient servants. In truth, Lewis's love of hierarchy is worth its own book, and somebody ought to write it.

FT: So given those fundamental flaws, should we just not watch the films at all?

JR: I don't think that's feasible (though I hope the filmmakers find some new consultants for the remaining movies; there are plenty of fantastic Lewis scholars who could help). As it stands the movies are an unavoidable part of the world of Lewis now, and they do have some benefit in driving newcomers to the books (and I hope, farther away from the films themselves).

That said, I do think parents who care about this sort of thing should be wise in how and when they introduce the movies. The danger of the films, especially for children, is the potency of the visual image. I've read *The Lord of the Rings* a few times, but I don't know them as well as I know Narnia. Because of that, it's hard for me to think of Frodo and not think of Elijah Wood, or to think of Samwise and not want to start chanting "Rudy! Rudy!" We often think in pictures, and a distorted movie can impress distorted pictures on our minds.

Funny story about the power of the visual image: There's a scene in Mel Gibson's *The Passion of the Christ* in which a Pharisee objects to Jesus's trial before the Sanhedrin on the grounds that only a select few of the members have been invited. He's immediately shouted down by the rest. I think such an idea fits well with my own biblical judgment that the Palm Sunday crowds are different people from the mob yelling "Crucify him!" The reason the Sanhedrin grab and accuse Jesus at night is because they know that many people in Jerusalem revere him as a prophet and would have a serious problem with their attempt to kill him. Anyway, I internalized the scene from the movie because it fits with my interpretation of the passage, and one day referenced the man's objection to a college class on the death of Jesus. The students looked at me with puzzled expressions and asked where that was in the Gospels. We spent fifteen minutes looking for it before I realized that I'd transposed the scene from the movie into my understanding of the Bible. The reason it worked is that Gibson's addition fit so seamlessly with my reading of the Gospels (at least at that point). Thus, the power of the image to affect the way we read.

Thankfully, the portrait of the Narnian characters in the films is so flawed and so unlike their counterparts in the books that they probably won't stick, especially for those who really love Lewis's originals. I expect that even children will be able to spot the differences, especially if their parents draw attention to them.

In saying all of this, of course, I'd also reiterate that I wouldn't presume to judge parents who let their children see the movies first. The key is that they aim for their kids to be discipled by the books and not the films. Those two roads diverge in the Narnian woods, and the one you choose will make all the difference.

Recommended Resources on Narnia

FT: Finally, could you recommend any other books that you've found especially helpful in understanding and appreciating Narnia?

JR: Absolutely. Four books stand out to me. First, there is the pair of books by Michael Ward: *Planet Narnia: The Seven Heavens in the Imagination of C. S. Lewis* and its little popular-level cousin, *The Narnia Code*. I'd recommend the latter for lay people who want to grasp some of the hidden layers of meaning in the book, and the former for serious students who really want to understand the totality of Lewis better. The third book is *What I Learned in Narnia* by Douglas Wilson. It's similar to the present volume, though organized differently and emphasizing various things that I don't treat. I'd highly recommend it. And lastly, I'd recommend Paul Ford's *A Companion to Narnia*, which is essentially a reference dictionary that summarizes various aspects of the book.

Beyond that, my own institution, Bethlehem College and Seminary, has a small publishing house (BCS Press) that produces curricula on various theological topics. We offer a course that provides a way for people to study the Narnian books as a group using Ward's *The Narnia Code* and the Chronicles themselves. You can find it at www.bcspress.org.

FT: On that note, I will have to let you go; they're expecting me on the Dancing Lawn at noon, and I don't want to be late. Thank you so much for your time.

JR: My pleasure.

Notes

1. C. S. Lewis, "Sometimes Fairy Stories May Say Best What's to Be Said" in *On Stories and Other Essays on Literature* (New York, NY: Harcourt, 2002), 46.
2. Owen Barfield, *Owen Barfield on C. S. Lewis* (Oxford, England: Barfield Press UK, 2011), 121–122.
3. Lewis, "Sometimes Fairy Stories," 46–47.
4. C. S. Lewis, "Letter to Sophia Storr," in *The Collected Letters of C. S. Lewis*, Vol. 3 (New York, NY: HarperOne, 2007), 1113.
5. C. S. Lewis, *Letters to Children* (New York, NY: Scribner, 1996), 44–45.
6. Lewis, "Letter to Mrs. Hook," *Collected Letters*, Vol. 3, 1004.
7. Lewis, *Letters to Children*, 45.
8. Lewis, "Letter to Mrs. Hook," 1004.
9. C. S. Lewis, "On Three Ways of Writing for Children" in *On Stories and Other Essays on Literature*, 37.
10. Lewis, "On Three Ways of Writing for Children," 38.
11. Lewis, "On Three Ways of Writing for Children," 39–40.
12. Lewis, "On Three Ways of Writing for Children," 40.
13. Lewis, "On Three Ways of Writing for Children," 33.
14. Lewis, "Sometimes Fairy Stories," 48.
15. Lewis, "On Three Ways of Writing for Children," 33.
16. Peter Leithart, "Authors, Authority, and the Humble Reader" in

The Christian Imagination, ed. Leland Ryken (New York, NY: Shaw Books, 2002), 217.

17. All quotations are from C. S. Lewis, *The Abolition of Man* (New York, NY: Simon and Schuster, 1996). Page numbers in parentheses.

18. Lewis, "Sometimes Fairy Stories," 47.

19. Peter Leithart, *Deep Comedy: Trinity, Tragedy, and Hope in Western Literature* (Moscow, ID: Canon Press, 2008).

20. C. S. Lewis, "The Necessity of Chivalry" in *Present Concerns*, ed. Walter Hooper (Orlando, FL: Harcourt Brace Jovanovich Publishers, 1986), 13.

21. Lewis, "The Necessity of Chivalry," 14.

22. Lewis, *The Abolition of Man*, 83.

23. Lewis, *The Abolition of Man*, 85.

24. G. K. Chesterton, *Orthodoxy* (New York, NY: Barnes & Noble, Inc., 2007), 45.

25. Chesterton, *Orthodoxy*, 44.

26. John Piper, "Clyde Kilby's Resolutions for Mental Health and for Staying Alive to God In Nature," italics original. This article may be found by performing a title search at www.desiringgod. org.

27. The image of the red lizard is taken from *The Great Divorce* (New York, NY: HarperOne, 2009).

28. For a comparison of the two versions of this scene, see Appendix Four, "Variances in the Ending of Chapter Twelve, 'The Dark Island,' in *The Voyage of the Dawn Treader*" in Paul Ford, *A Companion to Narnia* (New York, NY: HarperOne, 2005), 471–472.

29. C. S. Lewis, "The Humanitarian Theory of Punishment" in *God in the Dock: Essays in Theology and Ethics*, (Grand Rapids, MI: William B. Eerdmans Publishing Company, 1970), 294.

30. Lewis, "The Humanitarian Theory of Punishment," 292.

31. Lewis, "Is Progress Possible?" in *God in the Dock*, 313–314.

32. Lewis, "Delinquents in the Snow" in *God in the Dock*, 307.

33. C. S. Lewis, *The Screwtape Letters* (New York, NY: Touchstone, 1996), 7–8.

34. Lewis, "Is Progress Possible?" 316.

35. C. S. Lewis, *Mere Christianity* (New York, NY: HarperCollins, 2001), 52.

36. A fine summary of the views of Feuerbach and Freud may be found in Richard Lints, "The Age of Intellectual Iconoclasm: The Nineteenth-Century Revolt against Theism" in *Revolutions in Worldview: Understanding the Flow of Western Thought*, ed. W. Andrew Hoffecker (Phillipsburg, NJ: P&R Publishing, 2007)

37. C. S. Lewis, "The Weight of Glory" in *The Weight of Glory and Other Addresses* (San Francisco, CA: HarperCollins, 2001), 31.

38. Lewis, *Mere Christianity*, 136–137.

39. Lewis, "The Weight of Glory," 32–33.

40. C. S. Lewis, *The Problem of Pain* (New York, NY: The Macmillan Company, 1970), 93.

41. Lewis, "Man or Rabbit?" in *God in the Dock*, 108–109.

42. Lewis, *The Screwtape Letters*, 42

43. Lewis, *The Screwtape Letters*, 7.

44. Lewis, *Mere Christianity*, 127–128.

45. Lewis, *Mere Christianity*, 128.

46. C. S. Lewis, *Surprised by Joy: The Shape of My Early Life* (Orlando, FL: Harcourt Brace & Company, 1955), 18

47. Lewis, *Surprised by Joy*, 19.

48. Lewis, *Surprised by Joy*, 19.

49. Lewis, *The Abolition of Man*, 67.

50. Lewis, *The Abolition of Man*, 69.

51. Lewis, *The Abolition of Man*, 73.

52. Lewis, *The Abolition of Man*, 67–68.

53. Lewis, *The Abolition of Man*, 83.

54. Lewis, *The Abolition of Man*, 83–84.

55. "Bulverism" is a logical fallacy in which a person simply assumes that his opponent is wrong and then proceeds to

demonstrate this by explaining the origins of his belief. Lewis explores this fallacy in "Bulverism" in *God in the Dock: Essays in Theology and Ethics*, 271–277.

56. Lewis, "Letter to Dom Bede Griffiths," *Collected Letters*, Vol. 3, 111.
57. Lewis, "Myth Became Fact" in *God in the Dock*, 65–66.
58. Lewis, *The Screwtape Letters*, 42.
59. C. S. Lewis, *A Grief Observed* (New York, NY: Bantam Books, 1976), 6–7.
60. Lewis, *A Grief Observed*, 55–56.
61. Lewis, "Priestesses in the Church?" in *God in the Dock*, 235.
62. Lewis, "On Three Ways of Writing for Children," 34.
63. Lewis, *Mere Christianity*, 113.
64. S. M. Hutchens, "Fixing Lewis." *Touchstone Magazine*, November/December 2010.
65. Lewis, *Letters to Children*, 52.
66. Lewis, *Mere Christianity*, 175.
67. Lewis, *Mere Christianity*, 176.
68. Lewis, "Membership" in *The Weight of Glory and Other Addresses* (San Francisco, CA: HarperCollins, 2001), 168.
69. Lewis, "Equality" in *Present Concerns*, ed. Walter Hooper (Orlando, FL: Harcourt Brace Jovanovich Publishers, 1986), 18.

Related Ministries

Bethlehem College and Seminary

Bethlehem College and Seminary is an institution of higher education located in Minneapolis, MN. Under the authority of God's inerrant word, we exist to spread a passion for the supremacy of God in all things for the joy of all peoples through Jesus Christ by equipping men and women to treasure Christ above all things, to grow in wisdom and knowledge over a lifetime, and to glorify God in every sphere of life.

As a church-based institution, all of our programs are woven into the life and ministry of Bethlehem Baptist Church. At the undergraduate level, we offer programs in Christian Worldview, Biblical and Theological Studies, and the History of Ideas, as well as a non-traditional Degree Completion Program in Theology. At the seminary level, we offer carefully sequenced Master of Divinity and Master of Theology programs for those called to vocational ministry as pastors, missionaries, elders, and scholars.

Find us on the web at http://www.bcsmn.org.

BCS Press

BCS Press is the publishing division of Bethlehem College and Seminary. We publish God-centered curriculum for adults within the local church. All of our curricula are designed to be Bible-saturated, theological, rigorous, and pedagogically effective. These curricula have been produced by and used in the context of Bethlehem Baptist Church and its educational ministry, The Bethlehem Institute.

Find us on the web at http://www.bcspress.org.